Now This Is the Truth

...and other lies

Now This Is the Truth

...and other lies

Tales from the Eastern Shore...*and more*

Hal Roth

Nanticoke Books

Vienna, MD 21869

Manufactured in the United States by Victor Graphics

ISBN 0-9762545-0-6

Published by Nanticoke Books, Vienna, MD 21869

Contents

Illustrations

Acknowledgments

Acknowledgments are always a bitter-sweet time for me—sweet to recognize the wonderful folks that have made the book possible through their many and varied contributions, and bitter because I know I am going to forget to include somebody.

I want to thank Publisher David Pulzone and Editor Anne Farwell of *Tidewater Times*, where these stories first appeared, for the freedom they have given me during the past eight years to do my own thing.

The cover illustration is adapted from a painting by Dawn Tarr, who is also the subject of the story "Yay for Art."

The late Richard G. Speck, professor of anthropology at the University of Pennsylvania, took the photograph on page 79 of Lydia Clark's monument in 1927.

The photograph of Fujiyama on page 96 appears through the courtesy of the Konishi Brewing Co., Ltd.

Richard Mather took the photograph of the author on page 105.

The photograph of the *President Warfield* on page 168 appears through the courtesy of the late P. S. Gornto.

The photograph of the *U. S. S. President Warfield* (IX-169) on page 168 is an official U. S. Navy photograph.

The photographs of *Exodus* 1947 on page 177 appear through the courtesy of the Haifa Port Authority, Israel.

The late Justus A. B. Cowles took the photograph of Pete on page 186.

The photograph of the hanging of Wish Sheppard on page 213 is from a period postcard.

The remaining photographs were taken by the author.

As always, I owe a large dept of gratitude to the staffs at the Dorchester County Public Library in Cambridge, MD, the Caroline County Public Library in Denton, MD, and the Worcester County

Public Libraries in Snow Hill and Pocomoke City, MD.

In addition to acknowledgments made in the stories themselves, contributors of information and material include Bob Booth, Helen Chappell, Alvin Coleman, John Goslee, Howard Harding, Jack Knowles, the Japan Travel Bureau, Sharon Moore and Pat Pigg.

My office is in more disarray than usual—if that is possible—from a fruitless search for the name and address of the gentleman who sent me the story on page 4 about Mr. Penn, the Rock Hall barber. If you are still out there and see this, please give me a call.

Sally Boden, Toni Burns, Lisa Jo Frech and Sylvia Roth—valued friends all—have read parts of the book and advised and corrected me on numerous issues, and Elsie Smith has suffered through all 224 pages and helped to fine tune the finished product. Any goofs that remain are mine alone.

And thanks to Ken Saylor for lots of things.

Hal Roth,
Vienna, MD
September 2004

Now This Is the Truth

Have you ever noticed that when people tell you a story you suspect might be a huge, elaborate lie, they usually make a special effort to qualify it as the truth? Narratives are frequently punctuated with admonishments like: "Now this is the truth," "It's the truth, so help me God," or "My mother told me that, and she wouldn't lie."

Pay heed to my caution that it's never wise to display even the slightest facial distrust after the latter proclamation, especially if the narrator has larger biceps than yours.

"An old man used to help me sort 'maters and cultivate and stuff," a fellow told me one day in a country store. "He was livin' by hisself, and he told me one mornin', 'Yep,' he said, 'I slept in that bed all winter. I felt that knot down there in the end of that bed—felt that knot with my feet every night, but I didn't pay no attention to it. Come to find out it was a big old blacksnake layin' back in there.' All winter long that snake laid in them covers there with him. It made cold chills run down my back."

When the gentleman took notice of my expanding grin, he ruffled a little and indignantly defended his story: "No, it's the truth! He told me."

Did he really believe that a snake would have hibernated

1

through the winter in the warmth of the old man's bed? For many, an earnest and straight-faced rendering of a tale is the primary qualification that distinguishes between fact and fancy.

Here are a few of the many yarns I've been told in an atmosphere of complete candor. I'll let you judge the veracity of each. All I can say in support of them is to repeat the qualification offered by the man in the country store: "He told me."

•

Now this is the truth; it was told to me by my daddy. I've heard it told different ways, but this is the way it happened.

My daddy was workin' on a schooner that John Parker Sharp had. It was about seventy or eighty feet long, and he would lay it up with oysters in Chincoteague and sail up to the Connecticut River to the Connecticut Oyster Company. When they came back, they would reload with bricks or lumber. This was back when my daddy was about twenty years old.

Pop used to work on there with his cousin Ranzaloew Booth. This one time my daddy had scarlet fever, and so it was just Park and Ranzaloew. They went up and unloaded their oysters, and it was gettin' ready to have a bad storm; there was a heavy nor'easter comin' in. They unloaded right quick and deck-loaded some lumber and strapped it down. They didn't put it in the hold like you should.

Usually, as soon as they got out in the ocean, they'd throw the anchor and lay there that night and take off sailin' the next day; but when they headed back this time, the wind started blowin' a gale nor'east and the tide was runnin' down the beach. Ranzaloew said, "When are we gonna anchor? I'm nearly dead."

Captain Park said, "We're headin' south. We got a fair wind and a fair tide, and we got a storm comin'. You get up on the bow and stand watch."

They mackerel fished then, just like they do now, and for mackerel fishin' they had nets out. You had to keep watch so you didn't run across one and hang up.

So Ranzaloew got up on the bow, and he's up there about an

2

hour and comes back. "Cap'n Park," he says, "damn if I ain't nearly dead. Come on, let's anchor up and go below and get some sleep."

Park said, "No sir! We got a fair wind and a fair tide. You get up there and take care of your end and I'll take care of mine."

Another hour went by and Ranzaloew come back again. "Cap'n Park, I can't stand it no longer," he says; "let's anchor up and get some sleep."

Park said, "Shut up, and get up there and take care of your end. I've got mine."

So Ranzaloew went back up there, and about that time she rolled over on her side and the lumber capsized all over the deck. Park went runnin', and he yells, "What'd we hit? What'd we hit?"

Ranzaloew said, "We ain't hit nothin'. I anchored my end and I'm goin' to bed. You can damn well do what you please with your end."

•

I know you heared 'bout that great old snake used to live there to Peters' Swamp. You wrote 'bout it in a book one time—how that old man thought he set down on a log, but it was that great old snake he set on, and he had eyes big as saucers—I mean the snake did.

Well, you know, that old snake finally got killed up in a fire or I guess he'd still be livin' today. Clyde, one time, he was burnin' trash there to his place and the fire got away and caught that swamp up. It was a dry year anyway.

All the deers and stuff run out of it, but that old snake was nappin', I s'pose; and he weren't all that fast, neither, I don't guess, what with no legs and all that weight. They said he was big 'round as a pine tree.

So he done got burned up in the fire, and now that's the truth. Clyde's boy saw the carcass in there after everything cooled down.

All of that was a while back, you know, but I always wondered if that skull might still be in there someplace. Now wouldn't you like to have that to make a picture and put it in a book?

3

•

I'm eighty-one years old now, and when I lived in Rock Hall before World War II, there was a barbershop there called the Penn Barbershop. Here is a true story about him.

A state police came in one day and wanted a haircut and a shave, and he said to Mr. Penn: "You had better not cut me while shaving me or I'll kill you."

Mr. Penn was very good with a razor, and he could cut a fly in half, right out of the air.

Just as the state cop sat in the chair, a fly went by, and Mr. Penn swung that razor and cut it in half.

The cop said, "Never mind the shave, just give me a haircut."

•

Now here's a true story to show you how all this weather fore-castin' goes on. It was come fall one year, and the Indians on the reservation asked their new chief if the winter was gonna be cold or mild. They wanted to know, you understand, how much wood they needed to gather. Since the new chief had growed up in the modern world, nobody never taught him the old secrets. He could look at the sky and the trees and the animals, and he didn't have a notion what the weather was gonna be. So he decided to be on the safe side, and he told his tribe the winter was gonna be cold and they should collect enough firewood to be prepared.

After thinkin' about the whole matter for a couple days, he went to a phone booth in town and called the National Weather Service, and he said, "Are you predictin' a cold winter or a mild winter?"

"It looks like this winter's gonna be pretty cold," the man said.

So the chief went back to the reservation and told his people they had better collect even more wood to be sure they'd have enough.

A week later, he called the National Weather Service again. "Are you predictin' a very cold winter?" he asked the man.

"Yes," the weatherman says, "we're thinkin' it's gonna be a very cold winter. We seen more signs of it lately."

The chief went back to his people again and told 'em to collect every scrap of wood they could find.

Several more weeks went by and the chief was still worried, so he made another call. "Are you absolutely sure the winter's gonna be very cold?" he asked.

"Absolutely!" the man told him. "We have good reasons to believe it's gonna be one of the coldest winters ever."

"How do you know that?" the chief asked.

The weatherman says, "Because the Indians are collectin' wood like crazy."

•

There's a dead stock removal service, and their phone number is 1-800-DEADCOW. When you call there, they tell you to write a check, put it in an envelope and leave the envelope in the dead cow's mouth. That's the truth now; you couldn't make somethin' like that up!

•

It was on a Friday and it was possibly goose season; I don't remember for sure. I was waitin' at the wood yard for Avery and the wood dealer, and the geese were flyin' up and down the river real high. I looked up, and I never saw the like of geese in my life.

So Avery come, and he said, "They're flyin'."

I said, "Yep, I'll be right back. I'm goin' home and get my Mauser rifle and get one of them geese."

He said, "Are you kiddin'? They'll be a mile away, high and all."

I said, "I don't care."

So I come back, and there was a bunch floppin' behind. No sense to the way they were flyin', but there were three lead geese, one right behind the other. I said, "Well, I'll tell you what I'm gonna do. I'm gonna shoot at the first one's head, and the bullet should

5

split the breastbone in two of the middle one."

So I shot, and Avery said, "Ah, you missed; you didn't get either one."

And about that time the old second goose—his wings just fell right down, and here he comes a-hittin' the water. He was clear down from the wood yard.

There's a buoy over on the Dorchester side at what they call Myrkle [Myrtle] Bend Creek, and there was a tugboat comin' up the river pushin' an oil barge.

My neighbor Emerson was there and he said, "I seen where he fell."

The tide was runnin' in and Avery said, "You and Emerson run up to the wharf and get my skiff, and by the time you get it and go out there, that goose should be up there to the buoy."

So, 'bout the time I got out there, the tugboat captain pointed right where he was at. That bullet had split his breastbone open just like you took a knife and cut it. I said, "Emerson, you clean it for half of it."

With his height and everything, we estimated—Avery was good at that—that goose was a good half-a-mile away, and that was with an open sight. I could shoot that thing, and it was dead accurate. Wherever you put her, it would go there. I still got the rifle.

Sometimes I tell it that the goose was so far away I had to put salt on the bullet so the goose wouldn't spoil till I got there, but then you'd know it was all a lie. But that's the truth what I just told you.

•

Now here's a true story: A big-time lawyer from the city come down to Hoopers Island one time to hunt ducks. He rented a boat and a blind and set out a whole mess of decoys.

A little while after he gets there, this black duck comes along and the lawyer shoots it. But the duck falls on the marsh across the creek, so the lawyer has to get in his boat and paddle over there. He no sooner steps out on the marsh than an old man shows up.

"What are you doin' on my marsh?" the old man says.

"I shot a duck and it fell in that grass back there," the lawyer says.

"Well," the old man says, "I don't allow no trespassin' on my marsh. You'll have to leave."

"Look," the lawyer says, "I'm the best lawyer in Baltimore, and if you don't let me get my duck, I'll sue you and take every blade of grass you got in this marsh and then some."

"Ain't no need to go to all that trouble," the old man says. "We got a way to settle small disagreements down here. We call it the 'three-kick rule.'"

"And what would that be?" the lawyer says.

"Well," the old man says, "it goes like this: Since you're the trespasser, I get to kick you three times; then you get to kick me three times. And it goes back and forth like that until one of us gives up."

The lawyer is forty and he works out regular. The old man has to be at least seventy. "O.K.," the lawyer says, "let's see what you can do."

Before the lawyer can even brace himself, the old man plants a boot in his groin, doublin' him over. The second kick goes in the lawyer's midsection, droppin' him all the way to his knees, and the third comes from behind and sends him sprawlin' face down in the muck.

The lawyer lays there moanin' a while. Finally, he pulls hisself together and slowly gets up. "All right, old man, now it's my turn."

"Nah," the old Honker says, "I give up. You can have the damn duck."

•

Everybody thinks it's a lie when you tell how many ducks there was in the marsh one time, but it's the honest-to-God truth; they used to be thick as blackbirds in a cornfield. My brother and me used to hunt a little pond down below, just a spit or two off from Island Creek.

We went there in January one time, and it come up cold like you never seen it—I mean real sudden like.

We'd been settin' in the blind a spell when some black ducks pitched in. I was gonna take 'em but my brother said, "No, let's wait till some more come along."

So we set there a spell longer, and that's when it started to get cold.

Then some more ducks come in and I said, "Let's take 'em now."

"Nah," my brother said, "let's wait till a few more come along." So we set there some more, and it just kept gettin' colder and colder.

Every now and again, some more ducks would pitch, but my brother always said to wait a spell longer so we could get more when we'd shoot.

Well, that went on for about an hour or two: The ducks a-pitchin' and us a-waitin', and it getting' colder and colder by the minute.

Finally, there weren't enough room left in that pond for neither another duck, and my brother says, "O.K., let's take 'em."

But what we didn't know, you see, is that pond had froze right solid through, and all them ducks had their feet stuck in the ice. So when we jumped up outa that blind to shoot, them ducks took off and carried that whole pond right away from there.

Come the next tide, the pond filled in again, but we had to move the blind. The ducks remembered how they'd got froze fast and they never would pitch in there again after that.

A Lynched Man's Hand

"O...that I could forget what I have been." —William Shakespeare

On April 30, 1883, an unnamed journalist wrote in the *Denton* (MD) *Journal:* "I drove out yesterday to a tree, four miles from the village, which still bears the imprint of the hand of a Negro, which was nailed there by one of the mob that hanged, quartered, mutilated and burned him nearly twenty years ago. This singular freak of nature or sign manual of divine displeasure, as many residents of the county esteem it, is generally treated with such contemptuous disbelief by strangers visiting Caroline County that it is difficult to find one who has seen it willing to talk about it, but an official of the county, who did his full duty in an endeavor to stay the fury of the mob, consented to show me the remarkable tree. It is a giant swamp poplar, quite three feet in diameter, standing close by the road that opens up Tuckahoe Neck, the garden spot of the country. About twelve feet from the ground, on the road face of the tree, is a seeming scar, which might attract a casual glance on account of its marked difference in color from the other bark. Probably a stranger would not notice the singular tracing of which it is a frame, but to one looking for it, the outline of a human hand, somewhat elongated by the growth of the tree, grows as one looks until it takes almost the very similitude of the withering hand that was nailed there twenty years ago. Even the nail is still visible, although the bark has grown beyond so that it is half an inch below the surface. The tracing of the hand appears in a much smoother as well as lighter colored bark—the palm through which the nail was driven being clearest in shape, with the thumb and spread index and little finger scarcely less perceptible. My guide said the appearance grows more noticeable with each year, and it would be difficult to persuade him that it was not due to other than providential design. It is worthy of remark, lest the imprint in the tree be attributed to some action of the decomposing animal tissue, that lumbermen working in the vicinity made up a purse and hired a man to take the hand down within a week of the time it was placed there."

Ellen Plummer was the twelve-year-old daughter of Edgar Plummer, a successful farmer from near Greensborough in Caroline County, Maryland. On a Monday evening in the fall of 1863, Ellen failed to return home, having last been seen passing a densely wooded area that bordered the pathway between her school and residence. A search party discovered her body the following morning, deep in the forest and partially hidden beneath a heavy log. She had been sexually assaulted and brutally murdered.

Jim Wilson was described as a bright, young, mulatto male of twenty-three, the foreman on a small neighborhood farm and the "protector" of two maiden ladies. The citizens of Greensborough generally held him in high esteem as a trustworthy, polite and hard working member of the community. Although he was not a suspect in the girl's murder, Wilson was known to have been working in the woods during the preceding afternoon, and investigators approached him in the hope that he might have observed something to shed light on the tragedy.

It is not clear whether the questioning of Wilson was conducted by officers of the law or by members of the community, nor am I aware of how the subject of Ellen's murder was broached. What has survived is a report that the young man "turned pale, trembled violently and seemed on the verge of fainting" when the girl's name was mentioned.

After denying that he had been anywhere near the woods or knew anything of the crime, Wilson's protests became inarticulate and irrational, and his status quickly changed from potential witness to suspect. After what is described as a "brief, further examination," the interrogators placed the young man under arrest and immediately began to transport him to the Caroline County Jail in Denton, eight miles distant.

As the procession headed south on the Greensborough-Denton Road, word spread of Wilson's apprehension, and a growing number of excited farmers threw down their tools and joined the caravan. In response to cries of "Lynch him," a few cooler heads urged restraint. Wilson's guilt had, they argued, not been established as a certainty.

"Let's settle it now," someone suggested, and the prisoner was suspended from a tree limb by his thumbs. After submitting to an hour or more of harassment and threats, the terrified man confessed that he had murdered the girl, having been prompted, he claimed, by the devil.

Somehow, the confession had a moderating effect on the mob's fury. Wilson was lowered to the ground and the company continued to Denton, where their captive was locked in the county jail.

Many Caroline citizens apparently believed that the acknowledgment of guilt might have been nothing more than the acquiescence of a terrified man doing what was necessary to survive the moment. They were willing to allow a trial to sort out the facts, but on Wednesday, Thursday and Friday following Wilson's incarceration, a small crowd gathered daily at the jail. The group was composed mainly of young, idle men, many of whom were regarded almost with terror by honest citizens of the community. As the week progressed, their threats against the prisoner became increasingly open.

Sheriff Saulsbury was well aware that the flimsy lockup, which also served as his home, could not withstand a determined assault. I have been unable to discover if he failed to seek the assistance of other agencies or if he did so and was unable to convince them of the growing danger. Some claim that he awaited developments with apprehensions that rivaled those of his prisoner.

Just at dark on the Saturday following Ellen Plummer's murder, twelve individuals, making no attempt to conceal their identity, approached the jail. Perhaps another fifty men and boys accompanied them, watching from the darkness.

Not a word was spoken. Thomas Lockerman simply stepped up to the front door with an axe, sledgehammer and wedge and broke it down in minutes. Wilson had been retained on the upper floor, and he could be heard uttering prayers to both God and man for mercy. When they reached his cell, the gang found him on his knees.

One of the attackers carried the noosed end of a rope that trailed fifty feet down the steps and out into the jail yard. The loop was fastened around the neck of the victim, who made no attempt to struggle, and he was carried to the stair landing, praying for mercy. At a signal, the rope tightened with a savage jerk. It is likely that Wilson was dead before he reached the foot of the stairs.

Through the jail yard and into the street, thence past the courthouse, Wilson was dragged at the rope's end, his murderers yelling so savagely, witnesses claimed, that timid citizens shuddered behind their barred doors.

A large sycamore tree stood at the foot of the courthouse yard. The rope was tossed over a convenient limb and Wilson's body was raised off the ground. Some had brought shotguns and pistols and for a brief time amused themselves by riddling the corpse with bullets and birdshot. One load from a shotgun eventually severed the rope and the body fell, which seemed to intensify the mob's fury.

A second noose was secured around the neck of the mutilated cadaver and it was dragged to a tree in front of an African American church. The intention was to suspend it there as a warning to the race. The site, however, was in full view of one of Denton's favorite saloons, and its proprietor negotiated with principals in the crowd to take their pleasures elsewhere. In response, the assembly gravitated to a small valley on the outskirts of town, where the misguided avengers would enact their most atrocious malevolence.

In the group that evening was a Delaware butcher named Greenwell, who had brought the tools of his trade. With alcohol flowing freely and to the accompaniment of ribald songs and horrid imprecations, Greenwell chopped the body into small pieces that were heaped on a funeral pyre of brush and logs and burned. "The orgies enacted around the blazing faggots would have been deemed disgraceful by savages," a reporter wrote.

One of the more involved accomplices that evening was George W. Vincent, who had carried a hatchet for use in breaking into the jail. Vincent retrieved Wilson's hands from the fire and employed his small axe to blaze a place on a large poplar tree standing nearby, in the middle of which he nailed one of the appendages.

When his wife responded "in a shrewish humor," as reported by a witness, Vincent threw the second hand into her lap. She, in turn, tossed the gruesome object back into the fire, where it burned with the other remains.

Although many good citizens of Delmarva denounced the atrocity, no witness was willing to step forth and testify before a grand jury, and not a single perpetrator ever felt the hand of human justice. But if we can believe the tales that have added a chapter to Caroline County lore, a vengeful, higher fist served fearsome retribution.

Within twenty-four hours of the bloody orgy, Vincent's wife suffered paralysis of the arm she had used to toss Wilson's hand into the fire. Vincent was shot through the lungs shortly afterward while robbing a black man on Denton Causeway and died of pneumonia.

Greenwell's customers deserted him. "He may butcher his meat with the same knife he used to carve Jim Wilson," they said, and he sold no more meat in Caroline County. Intoxicated, he fell under the wheels of a train at Seaford one day and had his right arm severed. During a later drunken spree he toppled into the Nanticoke River. Although help was near at hand and he never sank below the surface, the butcher was dead when his body was pulled to shore.

Marcy Fountain, uncle of the murdered girl, saw his fortune disappear and died a pauper, while James Barwick and Thomas Lockerman are reported to have perished in the agony of delirium tremens, a violent shivering brought on by alcohol excess.

If we can believe the tales, everyone directly associated with the lynching died either in agony or poverty with a single exception. James Long was reported alive in 1883, though then an object of scorn in his community. I have read that although the perpetrators were never prosecuted, their fates served as a meaningful lesson to the youth of Caroline County.

POSTSCRIPT: Thirty-two years later, on March 26, 1895, the brutally murdered body of thirteen-year-old Sallie Dean was found beneath a pile of brush in a woods near the crossroads community of Harmony, ten miles south of Denton. She had left home for school that morning and never arrived. Marshall E. Price, a twenty-three-year-old blacksmith who lived nearby, was eventually arrested, tried, convicted and sentenced to death by hanging for the crime.

On the night of July 2, 1895, while Price was awaiting an appeal of his conviction, a mob broke into the Denton Jail. A noose was placed over the convicted man's head and he was dragged through a pummeling, kicking crowd to a nearby tree. There, the rope was thrown over a branch and Price, already dead, was lifted by his neck as the crowd shouted three cheers for the sheriff and judges of the court. The assembly then dispersed, leaving its victim's lifeless body to twist in the darkness. This time the lynchers were masked. Again, no one was brought to justice in a court of law. Again, whether folklore or fact, we are told that each accessory came to a violent end.

Yay for Art

"**W**onderful, bright, brilliant, super, eye-catching, whimsical, romantic, sexy, fun, funky, wild, crazy, slashy, impressionistic, contemporary, totally original, totally ahhhhhh!"

Could such a variety of acclaim have been heaped upon one young woman...upon one young woman's art?

The adjectives listed above constitute only a small handful of the praises sung for the paintings and other artistic creations of Delmarva native Dawn Tarr, and I have heard most of the same superlatives applied to the lady as well—especially brilliant, wild and wonderful. And what greater compliment could anyone pay to the artistry of someone who truly paints for the "everyman" among us than to say: "It fits like a pair of your favorite jeans."

Dawn Tarr is a bold and fearless lady and a bold and fearless artist. She is intensely expressive in her speech, in her gestures when describing things and in her art, but when asked to profile herself in words, she once made what surely ranks among the most concise autobiographical evaluations in history: "Prolific," she replied, and that may be the only time in her life when this loquacious creator has ever been so concise about anything.

But the appraisal is a good one; Dawn Tarr is, indeed, prolific. I know artists who consider themselves rushed if they produce a painting or two in a week. Among others the creative juices flow even more slowly.

"How long does it usually take to complete a painting?" I asked.

"I try to do an average of twenty a week," came the startling reply.

Tarr creates with her moods and she creates constantly. "Creating is a disease," she says with a grin, "but it's better than a cold."

How many preschoolers have you known who made a career choice before entering the first grade and couldn't wait to grow up and get with it...and who never wavered from that goal?

"When did you begin painting?" I asked the Worcester County, Maryland, native.

"As far as art in general is concerned," Tarr replied without hesitation, "it started before kindergarten. While snooping through the attic at my grandmother's house one day, I came across an old spiral notebook with 'Harley Davidson' carefully colored on the cover. It had been my father's notebook when he was in school, and when I looked inside, I found the most realistic drawing of a pig I had ever seen. It wasn't a cartoon but looked like the pigs on the farm. I couldn't believe he drew it. I was stunned and determined I was going to do that.

"That day was my epiphany," Tarr continued in a serious tone. "From that day on, my doodles became important to me; I wanted to draw like that. From then on, my grandmother could no longer keep a sheet of paper in the house. I went through notebooks like water, drawing and scribbling, coloring and having the time of my life. You could find me sitting in the pigpen with the baby pigs, sketching. I would sketch my grandmother rocking my brother to sleep—anything and everything became subjects to draw. My friends who dropped by to play found it absolutely boring, and I knew I was on my own with this obsession."

Norman Henry Tarr, Jr. amazed his daughter again when he designed and constructed a Tiffany-style lamp that still hangs in the Tarr's kitchen.

"I watched him draw out and create his own stained glass lamp, and I'm still amazed at how wonderful it turned out. I knew then that I could create anything if I put my mind to it. Watching him was like magic. The radio would be playing country music, and the big hit song then was 'The Dukes of Hazard.' I would sing it to him while he worked.

"When I was in college, Dad switched from farmer to waterman. He does a lot of creative things," she said with pride. "He's a problem solver; he finds better ways of doing things.

"I was born and grew up in Snow Hill on a huge farm that's way back in the forest. 'Living back here,' Mom used to say, 'you can really tell who wants to see you.'

"I spent days building forts from hay bales with my brother, chasing kittens and snakes in the barn and doing tons of chores. It kept us healthy and grounded. Feeding the calves every morning and night was fun—mixing powdered milk in metal buckets and carrying four or five at a time to the stables. Helping the crew throw hay bales onto the giant trucks. Riding in the combine with my dad when he took in the corn crops. Chasing baby pigs. Gathering eggs. Picking strawberries and all the vegetables from the largest garden I have ever seen to this day. Riding bareback on the ponies my grandfather brought home.

"Pulling sweet corn was a major pastime in the summer, and I sold it on the side of the road at a dollar a dozen. I sat there and dreamed of selling my art that way. That's how I got my first truck. Picked 3,000 dozen. Yowza!" Tarr added for emphasis.

"A very interesting man came into my life at that time. His name was Howard Waters, an old black man who drove a very old, green car. He saw I was getting bad cases of sunburn, so he would come and get all the corn that could fit in his car and peddle it for me.

"One morning he came early, and I ran into the cornfield in my nightgown and was scorched by a fodder worm. It feels like a cigarette lighter being held against your skin. Howard took out a bottle of his 'pink alcohol,' as I like to call it. It was something he made with roots. He was always digging roots from the ditches. He poured it on the spot and the pain went away. That was the day I learned that magic really does exist. Howard was the most magical person I

17

ever met. He was in tune with so much, and I wanted to be in tune too.

"Howard was almost blind and he couldn't write. His voice was like a whisper, but he played piano with curled-up fingers and sang like a dream in old hymn-jazz ways. He died last Christmas at a hundred and six. He was the most fascinating man I ever met.

"Magic, creativity, dreaming, poetry, painting—all go hand in hand. If one is missing, the recipe isn't right.

"I didn't look forward to kindergarten. It took me away from the things I was familiar with and into the arms of people who didn't live the way I did—who lived in town, who had never touched a giant steer, who didn't have barns.

"But one day a poster contest rolled around and everything changed. I was determined and I won. That was the beginning of the monster.

"Then there was a film festival in elementary school. It was wonderful. They took me into rooms with blank film, stop action cameras—so many foreign things—and they turned me loose with the equipment. I wrote a story and read it into a tape recorder. I was allowed to create and create. I remember it so clearly: taking wax pencils and drawing on rolls of film and cutting and making paper figures. It was amazing. Time stood still there.

"Later that year some teachers came to me and said I had to go to Baltimore for a film festival; I had been chosen to be part of a competition. I couldn't figure out why they liked my story. I thought it was dumb, but I had so much fun creating. I think it won honorable mention.

"I encountered my first real art teacher in middle school: Christy Powell. She was awesome. I learned oil painting, and that was a huge transformation. Mrs. Powell's mother is Myrna McGrath, the Eastern Shore artist who does those wonderful maps of the Chesapeake Bay and who eventually became a close friend and mentor. When I turned sixteen, she taught me a lot about watercolor in exchange for cutting mats, which I was horrible at.

"One day I was running on top of a big barrel as it rolled down a hill. I was getting pretty good at it, but on the third run I fell and broke my right wrist—my drawing hand. The doctors told me I would never draw again, but Mrs. Powell sent me outside with pencil and sketchbook as soon as the cast was off. I can't thank her enough.

"Then came high school. To be honest, I hated it. The only good thing was the Snow Hill Band. I loved twirling that huge flag, going to parades and performing, seeing the looks on people's faces when we had our routine together.

"When senior year rolled around, I left and went to Pocomoke High. Mr. Buchanan, the art teacher there, was all I had ever dreamed. He had a kiln, and I began sculpting in clay like a mad woman, and I painted murals in the gym. I was never so scared in my life. I had never painted on such a scale before.

"Graduation day came and Columbus College of Art & Design in Ohio offered me a scholarship. Mr. Buchanan told me: 'Ill kick your butt all over the Eastern Shore if you don't go.' So I did.

"CCAD was a new world. The classes were really difficult and tested your ability to accept criticism. Instructors would tear your work to shreds and do a dance on the pieces, and they would yell: 'This isn't good enough to line a cat box! What were you thinking?'

"It was the most humiliating experience. People like myself, who had been painting since they were five and had been told 'Oh, that's lovely' by teachers all their lives, suddenly got a reality check. My first day I was deemed 'champion of wrongness.' I listened, bit my lip and redid the projects. I lived on No Doze and coffee and chocolate covered coffee beans, and I kept a job at night.

"I learned a lot there. The instructors crammed information into you and kept you awake at night. I still cringe when I hear the alarm go off because I think I'm late for a class. If you missed one assignment, you failed.

"There were four classes or more a day, and each of them required a finished product almost every week: full sculptures, oil paintings, life drawings—you name it. Then there were the dreaded art history classes. I took a tiny tape recorder with me in case I fell asleep.

"Most of the students ended up working for Nickelodeon, Disney, Hallmark and other industries. I never, ever, had the desire to do that. I refuse to deal with people who give you stipulations. There are no stipulations in art; it's wide open. I don't feel I should bend my style or my life to a corporation who sees you as a number. They take your ideas and make the cash, and you're paid by the hour. Yeah, O.K., you know what your paycheck will be, but it's like highway robbery. You only live once and I have no desire to live in a cubicle. It sucks the soul out of you. So I did what was best for my soul: I left and moved back home. I was one year from graduation.

"To my parents dismay, I didn't jive with Salisbury University. It's a great school, but I had been sculpting live, life-sized models for several years, and they wanted me to sculpt a doggy dish. So the thought of hanging in for an art teaching job flew out the window along with my parents' expectations for me to get a real, paying job.

"I moved to Chincoteague, Virginia, and it was like setting foot in a fairytale. I wrote a children's book but never had the chance to show it to anyone. I made good friends, spent most of my days painting names on workboats—painting the entire boats once a year and putting squid paintings underneath for the fish to see. Oops, that was a secret.

"I painted a mural at the Chincoteague Inn, which led to a few more. Tourists came to visit and I always had plenty to show and sell to them—lighthouses and ponies galore. My art can be seen in Memories Restaurant and on many horse trailers. Donna Leonard had T-shirts made from my work for the birdwatchers, and the Chincoteague Chapter of Ducks Unlimited named me Artist of the Year. I had a makeshift gallery in a restaurant and face painted all summer long.

"But times were tough around there. If you didn't make the money you needed to live on in three months, you were in trouble for the rest of the year.

"Gene Tolley came to my home one day and commissioned me to do a mural in his restaurant, The Beachway. I painted ponies across the wall with the Chincoteague lighthouse in the background.

"Life changed for me at that point. Gene and his wife, Shirley, took me in, and I worked in the restaurant; and eventually they moved me to Cambridge, where I opened The Break of Dawn Gallery. But I found that my creative juices didn't work as well in a public setting."

Dawn Tarr and Michael Tolley, Gene and Shirley's son, fell in love, and the couple moved to Toddville, surrounded by the great Dorchester marshes. "I love it here," Tarr told me. "The views are awesome!"

In Toddville, the Internet has become this enterprising artist's primary showcase. To view a sampling of her work, go to eBay, the Internet's premier auction site, and enter "Dawn Tarr" on the search line. Be sure to bookmark it because the art will change throughout each week. You can also visit Tarr's personal website at www.dawn-tar.com or see a selection of her creations at the Alternative Gift Gallery in Cambridge, or at Splash in St. Michaels, Maryland.

On eBay, a Tarr painting usually attracts from a hundred to six or seven hundred lookers, but once she drew seven thousand hits on an offering titled "Vagina Garden," which depicted a field of calla lilies. Sorry guys.

"Selling on eBay is more productive and entertaining than running a business or showing in galleries," she asserts. "I now have my life back."

And what is a typical day in the life of Dawn Tarr?

"Lots of coffee, big canvass, large paintbrushes and a very understanding man who allows me to totally wreck the house. Sometimes I paint outside and throw paint everywhere. Way too much fun!

"I know it sounds like a horrid life to some, but I couldn't be happier. This is all I ever wanted to do as a child, and what do you know, its working! If van Gogh could see me now!" Tarr shares a birth date with the famous impressionist Vincent van Gogh.

"You must need to escape sometimes," I suggested. "Where do you go when you've had enough of it?"

"Art *is* my escape. I go into that world and ignore everything else." Then she paused for a few seconds, smiled and added: "Cool!"

"I would love to start an artists' island out here, build little cabins or buy up the houses and have all my artist friends move here. Then all the shops could come and purchase art at wholesale prices. No artist would have to live in a van or go hungry or be cold again. Believe me, I've seen those days."

Tarr likes to paint big, wielding her brush with bold slashes. She creates striking images from what appears to be an inexhaustible well of ideas. If you don't like what she delivers today, wait until tomorrow; it won't be long before you fall in love with a dozen of her paintings.

And what are the subjects that Tarr chooses to immortalize? Absolutely everything our blue dot in space has to offer...and a few things that are not of this world. My seven-year-old granddaughter has most recently fallen in love with "Monsters Brushing," a collection of the most unlikely critters you have ever seen, each scrubbing its teeth—or tooth—in preparation for bedtime. Nothing is off limits to Tarr's brushes.

"Where do you find the inspiration for all of this," I asked in awe.

"I have no idea," the tall redhead humbly replied. "It just comes to me."

Although she speaks with wild enthusiasm about her life and career, Tarr is very humble about her work and treats each sale as a gift making it's way into the world. Buyer satisfaction is primary to her business.

Tarr's vehicle of choice is a jeep with lifts and mud tires and flares and a sign on the back that reads "Break of Dawn."

"Are the lifts for looks or to keep your butt out of the high tides that often cover the roads down here?" I inquired.

"Both," she replied. "It's a bad machine and I'm totally loving the look. It's so funny; all the boys turn and stare when I ride through town. They're surprised to see a girl driving it."

Tarr is full of surprises, and they all come with a gleam in her eye. "You know what I'd really like to try?" she told me near the end of our chat: "Singing! I burst into song all the time. It embarrasses the people I'm with. I can pretty much sing along with any song, old or new. Love jazz. It's this year's back-of-my-mind dream. We'll see."

22

And how would I sum up Dawn Tarr's life so far?

I think I'd borrow one of her favorite exclamations: "Yay for art!"

Dawn Tarr

Blowing My Chance
for Fame

Opportunity always knocks twice, I was once told, as opposed to the single rap we are generally promised. I can only hope it's true, but I suspect that if it does for me, it will be the kind of opportunity that Mark Twain had in mind when he advised us to always acknowledge our mistakes, thereby throwing others off guard and giving us the opportunity to commit more.

In today's fast-moving and multi-dimensional world, one needs to remain vigilant. Opportunities can present themselves at the most unexpected moments and in the most unlikely places. They may appear while you are sipping coffee in your recliner and watching the evening news. They can be lurking behind the simple ring of a telephone. We must remain constantly prepped in anticipation of our call to the plate, and when the moment of truth arrives—well, good reader, you need to keep a clear head on your shoulders so you don't let the chance slip away like I did.

They say that everyone will enjoy at least fifteen minutes of fame in a lifetime. As shameful as it is for me to admit, I'm about to tell you how I threw away the opportunity to bask for an entire hour in the glowing spotlight of public esteem—worldwide, at that.

It was Monday and I was watching the CBS Evening News. Dan Rather was droning on about the latest Middle-East crisis when my phone rang. The well-modulated voice on the other end of the line informed me that I was speaking to Clayton Willis, talk show host of Radio Station WPBR in West Palm Beach, Florida. It went on to inform me of Mr. Willis' connections to the Eastern Shore and somewhat immodestly led me to understand that he was not just some run-of-the-mill personality. To insure that my comprehension had been perfected, names like Larry King were injected into the overview: "It's like *Larry King Live*; I'm sure you've seen that show."

The voice next dropped the names of a well-known Eastern Shore politician and popular restaurant that had, it claimed, been the objects of attention on a Clayton Willis radio show that very day. I shall refer, hereafter, to the individual and place of business as "[The Politician]" and "[The Restaurant]" respectively.

Next, some of my books were mentioned: *Conversations in a Country Store* and "*You Still Can't Never Get to Puckum.*"

I informed the voice that in the latter case it had combined two books into one title: *You Can't Never Get to Puckum* and *You Still Can't Get to Puckum.*

The voice told me that it had seen the latter and had heard good things about *Conversations.*

After striving to build up my ego for several minutes more, the voice finally got around to the point of the call: It wanted me to participate in a live radio interview on Wednesday.

Sorry, I had other commitments on Wednesday.

Well, Thursday would be O.K.. The hour-long discussion would be conducted and broadcast through some sort of telephone hook-up.

I wanted to know what subjects would be discussed, and when I didn't get a satisfactory answer, I inquired again.

"You keep asking that question," the voice said in a rather argumentative tone.

"That's because I haven't received an answer to it," I replied firmly.

When I still didn't get one, I suggested that Patty Cannon might provide a subject of interest for the voice's listeners. It hadn't heard of Patty and her gang of cutthroats, so I offered a brief overview. A mild interest was expressed and I shall pick up the conversation verbatim from that point.

"Well, anyway, how are we gonna do this. You wanna try and do this?"

"I'll give it a try, but you're taking a chance on me if it's done live and I don't know what I'm going to talk about ahead of time."

"Not in the slightest bit, but there's a—uh, can you toss in a few dollars for this?"

"I beg your pardon."

"I pay my station. I buy the hour, and then I have to run around and sell the thing—get people to buy ads or pay to be on the thing."

"Well, I'm certainly not going to pay to be on it."

"That's the problem. People never understand this, but independent stations operate like this. A lot of them have sales staffs of their own, but my station does not. They have one guy that does some little stuff that doesn't amount to anything. So what's-his-name, [the owner of The Restaurant], gave me some money this morning and then he had me to dinner. So, what I charge is four hundred bucks an hour, but Lord, I'd do it for a hundred dollars just to do it—get the word out. I think it would be an interesting thing—be helpful to the area. A lot of people come through here."

"Well, I'm afraid I'm not going to be able to help you."

"What?"

"I'm not going to pay to be interviewed."

"Well, people generally understand it [a minute ago, they didn't]. Well, O.K., I thought I'd give it a try. Maybe I can get [The Politician] on again. Do you know anybody that would like to do it?"

"How much did [The Politician] pay you?

"Well, he...he didn't. See, the...[The Restaurant] was the sponsor."

"I was pretty sure [The Politician] didn't pay you."

"Well, I don't know what he does, but I mean.... I got the—this business, you know.... [The Restaurant] will get an incredible amount of business from this thing because people—well, people listen in Israel. We get calls from Israel, from Bulgaria, from Venezuela—all over the world. So people get it. So, O.K. Well, I enjoyed talking to you."

It had to be a scam, I thought, but come on, there have got to be at least a million better ways to swindle people. I mean how many folks in the world are going to pay $400 to be interviewed, even if they can be heard in Israel, Bulgaria and Venezuela, but I was getting really curious. I hung up and called [The Politician].

"He says he's got a program in Florida and I think he's legit, but I don't think he's got any money behind him. He records by telephone and talks a mile a minute. He plugged [The Restaurant] constantly. I told him some stories. I try to promote the Shore however I can, even if it's done in Florida, but he didn't ask me for any money whatsoever."

I decided to drop the matter and booted up my computer to check for e-mail. The first message was from my book distributor.

"Clayton Willis," it began, "talk show host of radio WPBR in West Palm Beach Florida, called and left a very extensive message on our machine about you and your books. He was traveling through Maryland, saw your books somewhere and wanted to get in touch with you.

"He said we could call [The Restaurant] at [their number] or reach him at [a Palm Beach post office box number].

"He wanted us to send a copy of *Conversations in a Country Store* to the above address, gratis of course.

"We didn't, nor did we phone [The Restaurant], for what would we say to them? 'How's business?'

"We thought we would put this in your court, give you the appropriate info and allow you to contact Mr. Willis, as we can't speak for you, nor, I am sure, would you want us to."

I closed my e-mail and went to my favorite Internet search engine, typed in "WPBR Palm Beach Florida" and clicked on "Search."

Bingo! "Welcome to the All New WPBR 1340 AM the home of Omni-Lingual Broadcasting!

"1340 WPBR has provided the Palm Beaches with over 45 years of broadcasting excellence and tradition. 1340 WPBR prides itself on being the station in touch with the feelings and opinions of the residents of the Palm Beaches as well as providing entertainment and information for the diverse and distinct groups that make up the population of the Palm Beaches and surrounding counties.

"1340 WPBR's Talk Shows air Monday-Friday from 6 a.m. to 7 p.m., giving listeners the opportunity to voice their opinions and views to a local host on all types of issues and topics. These locally driven programs allow listeners to gain insight on issues that directly affect their own community in which they reside. National and International issues are also discussed, giving insight to local feelings on these National and International issues of concern.

"Evening and weekend programming includes musical entertainment, church programming, and the #1 rated French-Creole programming in all of South Florida. We are 1340 WPBR, The Station That Speaks Your Language! Click here to view our advertisers."

The site provided an opportunity to contact the station by e-mail. I filled in my name, address and telephone number, as requested, and wrote: "I received a telephone call this evening from someone claiming to be Clayton Willis, a talk show host on your station, and he attempted to solicit money from me to conduct an interview. Would you tell me, please, if this individual is known to you and if you are aware of such a practice?"

Then I noticed that WPBR also offered a variety of opportunities for further inquiry, and one of them was labeled the "Clayton Willis Talk Show." I clicked on the name bar.

A small, somewhat grainy photograph of a robust, past-middle-aged gentleman in a dark blue suit appeared. He was standing in front of a very impressive lectern and had an ID card dangling from a lanyard around his neck. You know the kind I mean: those plastic encased passes that you see hanging on everyone in the CIA and FBI movies.

In the background, a large oval sign was affixed to a royal-blue screen. It read: "THE WHITE HOUSE" and included an impressive facsimile of our presidential mansion mounted above the words.

The picture, I feel certain, has not won any photographic awards. The composition has been adjusted so that "THE WHITE HOUSE" commands a viewer's attention, with Mr. Willis off to the left side, facing the left border. But there was no missing the point that I was looking at one really important fellow, and the accompanying text verified that impression: "Clayton Willis, The White House Correspondent, Presidential Advisor, TV and Radio Broadcaster, Newspaperman, War and Crisis Correspondent, Critic, Art Collector, Sportsman, Lecturer and World Traveler, is host of the Willis Talk Show.

"It addresses political and social issues, the arts, sports and other current topics. Clayton Willis covers the world and the local scene from the Middle East, Rhodesian and Vietnam wars to the 2000 Election recount in Florida. He and his guests put you there in the action."

O.K., the man existed, but was it possible that the impressively-credentialed Clayton Willis of station WPBR, Omni Language Broadcasting in West Palm Beach, Florida, could be on the Eastern Shore of Maryland and trying to hustle money from a small-time regional writer?

Several days passed with no reply to my e-mail. I rooted out the web site again and dialed the telephone number listed there. A man's voice answered on the first ring.

"This is Hal Roth calling from the Eastern Shore of Maryland," I began. "There was a gentleman up here this past week soliciting money to do interviews for broadcast on your station. He identified himself as Clayton Willis and claimed to be one of your talk show hosts. It seems a little strange to me that someone from Palm Beach would have an interest in interviewing people in a rural area in Maryland, and even more strange that he would be asking for payment to do so. I was wondering if you could verify that this fellow really is whom he says he is."

I was transferred to the station manager, Virginia Martinez, and repeated my spiel.

"Yes, he does exist," Martinez told me, "but he's not here. He's been on a trip for the past few weeks."

"And does Mr. Willis charge people to interview them?"

"All of our programs are brokered. The hosts pay for their time, and if they do interviews, they charge for the interview. We do interviews from all over, not just necessarily in Florida. We're heard all over the world via the Internet."

Well, O.K., so I blew my chance for a whole hour of international fame. You might accuse me of talking sour grapes, but I view fame a little like Marlo Thomas, who once said, "Fame lost its appeal for me when I went into a public restroom and an autograph seeker handed me a pen and paper under the stall door."

And then there was John Dryden, who once observed: "Thy genius calls thee not to purchase fame?"

But hey, when you're dining out some evening at [The Restaurant] and suddenly find yourself surrounded by a hungry mob of Israelis, Bulgarians and Venezuelans, please do me a favor and ask if any of them know how to get to Puckum.

Old News

There are lots of ways to spend an evening: watching television, movies, theater, sports, reading the latest best seller, visiting with friends, downing a few at the local pub...but one of my favorites is curling up with an old newspaper. Old news can be addicting.

A century and more ago, much of local, regional, even national and international news was concisely reported in an almost run-on manner beneath small captions such as "Local Intelligence," "News of the Neighborhood," "News Gleanings," "Scraps" and "Dashes Here and There."

Most papers did not use bold, shouting headlines. Paper was scarce, and no editor wasted it with huge banners. Headlines were commonly the same size as the text, sometimes in a slightly bolder font or set in capital letters, and there was usually no extra space between the headline and the story. To find out what was on the page, you had to put your nose squarely into it.

Reporting was often very personal. You learned who had entertained visitors and who was out of town. If you painted your house, the event might make page one. Prejudices were openly expressed and juveniles were not spared from having their names publicly announced if they erred. Mail and steamboat schedules, poems, jokes, literary fiction, necrological notes (the obits) and more were scattered throughout the few pages. Sometimes it was hard to distinguish an advertisement from the news, and the line between them was often very gray.

The following random excerpts were taken from the *Denton* (Maryland) *Journal.*

Did you think lawyer jokes were something new? Guess again.

In the city of Halifax, there dwelt a lawyer, crafty, subtle and cute as a fox. An Indian of the Miamic tribe, named Simon, owed him some money. The lawyer had waited long for it. His patience at last gave out and he threatened the Indian with lawsuits, process and executions.

The poor red man got scared and brought the money to his creditor. The Indian waited, expecting the lawyer to write a receipt.

"Receipt," said Simon.

"Receipt?" said the lawyer. "What do you know about a receipt? Can you understand the nature of a receipt? Tell me the use of one and I will give it to you."

Simon looked at him a moment and then said: "S'pose maybe me die, me go to heben. Me find the gate locked. Me see the 'postle Peter. He say, 'Simon, what you want?' Me say, 'Want to get in.' He say, 'You pay Mr. J. dat money?'

"What me do I hab no receipt? Hab to hunt all over hell to find you!" —*6/7/1873*

ELOPERS COME TO DENTON TO WED: A dispatch from Laurel, Delaware, on Tuesday last said: "Eluding practically the entire force of State authorities and hundreds of Delaware residents, who had united to catch the pair, John H. Hall, 50 years old, and Alda May Horseman, 14 years old, daughter of Mr. and Mrs. William Horseman, of Laurel, eloped from the Horseman home early yesterday morning, secured an automobile, and speeding to Denton, Md., were married. They returned to Laurel late this afternoon and were taken into custody immediately. Hall was locked up in the town prison, which is now surrounded by a mob who threaten to do violence to the man. The girl is confined at the residence of Chief of Police Davis. The parents of the girl say they will prosecute Hall and have already taken action to have the wedding annulled."

The couple applied to Rev. G. L. Helsby, Denton, who after closely questioning each of them and talking with a young man here acquainted with them, performed the ceremony. The young woman gave her age as eighteen, but the young man who secured the license for the visitors gave it as twenty. The groom was a widower. The applicant for the license gave his age as thirty. —*1/27/1894*

Robes and blankets are very cheap at the Hardware on account of the warm weather.

The steamer Choptank has been withdrawn from the Nanticoke route for the winter.

Eggs were worth 12 cents a dozen early this week. The prices go up as the mercury goes down.

The county commissioners on Tuesday last appropriated $125 to assist in improving the streets of Greensborough.

On Friday evening of last week a "bonnet social" was given by the little folks of Hillsborough and Queen Anne at Hackett's Hall. The honor prize was won by Barton Chance.

A number of young Hillsborough people enjoyed a delightful straw-ride to Denton one evening last week.

The proprietors of Ridgely's new ice house are smiling this morning over the arrival of the expected cold wave. As yet, they have been unable to secure ice, owing to the open, warm winter. Visions of the Fourth of July and the demand about that time for something to cool fevered brows are evidently before them.

The streets of Federalsburg are much benefited by the shells already spread upon them, and the memory of the present board of county commissioners will be handed down to future generations with gratitude, if they will continue the good work.

The purchase of two additional street lamps was ordered for Denton—one for the southeast approach to town and the other for east Main Street.

Rev. J. W. Easley, Chestertown, was given a complete surprise recently by his congregation. Substantials were heaped upon his pantry shelves and a very enjoyable time was spent by the "Pounders." —1/ 27/1894

MR. GOSLIN'S LAW EFFECTIVE: "The new local option law, framed by State Senator Edward E. Goslin and enacted at the recent session of the General Assembly, it is claimed, has already greatly improved conditions in Caroline county," says a correspondent, writing in the Baltimore Evening Sun of Tuesday. "The 'wetness' at certain points in the county, which led to the enactment of this drastic measure, has disappeared, and the entire county is now said to be absolutely 'dry,' so far as the procuring of intoxicants within the county is concerned.

"More than thirty-four years ago, this county voted 'dry,' and there have been no legal sales of liquor, save for medicinal purposes only, here in that time. However, during most of that period, it has been comparatively easy to buy intoxicants in some form. More than one ingenious device to overcome the bar of the prohibition statute has been tried, with more or less success; but the advance in public sentiment has been gradual, and either by reason of this or of amendments to the local option law, violations have been reduced. In the early days of county prohibition, distilleries along the Delaware border and licensed saloons contiguous to the county lines made it comparatively easy for a considerable proportion of the bibulous population to secure ardent spirits.

"The steamboat barrooms were frequent havens to the thirsty of the territory along the Choptank River. But the licensed saloons have all gone, and with them the sale of liquor on steamboats plying the Choptank. The distilleries are now a negligible quantity, with the prohibition laws of the lower counties of Delaware. The 'social and literary club,' which once flourished in the towns with an enthusiastic membership, was in vogue only a few years, for public opinion would not stand for its real purpose, and grand juries had little difficulty in securing evidence against the 'literary fellers' who were its guiding spirits.

"The bootlegger flourished for a time, but the courts were apt to be severe upon him, and his patrons were rather untrustworthy. A certain class of the colored population took zealously to this traffic, and some scores of Caroline negroes are living—or have died—'in exile' in Smyrna, or Philadelphia, or Baltimore, as fugitives from indictments, while many of their fellows have been inmates of the House of Correction.

"At a time, drinks could be had as premiums for trivial purchases at stores, but this method of evasion was summarily done away with by amending the local option law to include 'giving away' in places of business as well as selling intoxicating beverages.

"The 'pear cider' and 'ambrosia' plague, so familiar in other 'dry' sections of Maryland, never amounted to much in Caroline. The selling of ordinary hard cider was fitfully pursued, and the negroes found that the addition of snuff made it highly desirable for intoxicating purposes, but few white men took to the combination. Jamaica ginger was another substitute for liquor, and from time to time some brand of 'bitters' or 'schnapps' would have a drug store run until public complaint was made of its effects upon the peace and sobriety of the community.

"Under the new law it is said that the county is 'dryer' than has been the case for many years. This act cuts out all the substitutes for liquor and also the prescription trade in 'spirtitus frumenti.' Under it there cannot be sold or given away in a place of business any liquor, medicated bitters or compound, the chief or principal ingredient of which is alcohol, or cider of any kind, by any person, firm or corporation, either directly or indirectly, by way of barter; nor can orders for such be taken within the county, under penalty of at least one year's imprisonment in the House of Correction for the first offense, and at least three years' imprisonment in the same place for every subsequent offense.

"Provision is made for the filing of information by the State's attorney in cases appealed from justices of the peace and for the prosecution of any one or more of the members of a firm or directors, trustees or managers of a corporation. It is generally thought that under the new law infractions must occur in the cases

35

of physicians and druggists in dispensing tinctures and other preparations required by the formulary to contain a major proportion of alcohol, although in practically all instances the character of the compound is such that it can hardly be used as an intoxicant; and it was for this reason that a number of professional men at the late term of court asked the judges for advice as to how far it would be safe for them to ignore the law. The judges, as a matter of course, would decide nothing in advance, but the impression holds with doctors and druggists that so long as the spirit of the act is observed, they are not likely to be bothered with its letter.

"A notable effect of the law, according to the physicians, is the total subsidence of stomach ache and other agonizing symptoms for the relief of which the sufferer was firmly convinced he needed whisky, and desired to be armed with a prescription. While under the old prescription law there has never been, it is asserted, any charges made before a grand jury against Caroline physicians of bad faith or judgment in giving prescriptions of this kind, nevertheless, as a matter of human experience, it was hardly possible for a doctor engaged in practicing medicine for a living and holding intimate personal relations with patients, past, present and prospective, to entirely escape being impressed at some time with a story of suffering and illness and pleaded with for the sovereign remedy admitted to the particular case." —*4/30/1910*

There is now a case before the Baltimore Superior Court, which serves as a reminder of slavery days. Samuel Jackson, colored, has sued Josiah H. Hughes, white, to recover $2,500, which sum the plaintiff paid to Hughes from 1849 to 1853 inclusive, at $48 a month. Jackson was free and was working to free his wife and children owned by Hughes. In 1853 Hughes declared that the wife and children should not go free, anyhow, and so Jackson lost his money, time and trouble.

Mr. Lee Davis met with quite a mishap at Fruitland one day last week. He left his wagon containing a large quantity of drugs (put up by J. H. Douglas of this place) on the railroad track while he was engaged in one of the stores for a few minutes with the proprietor.

He was soon informed of the fact that a passing train had run into his vehicle, quite demolishing it. He contrived, nevertheless, to bring it back yesterday, by borrowing a wheel. We noticed as he passed through town the wind playing merrily with the remainder of the curtains, while his countenance betrayed his unappreciativeness of the ludicrousness of the scene.

These cool chilly nights of September serve to warn lovers and all sentimental people that the time for leaning on gates to woo and taking charming strolls by moonlight has come to an end.

Last year the managers of the Delaware State Fair at Dover cleared $3,600, and this year they nearly doubled that amount.

Levin P. Rowland and William Atkinson, the Democratic and Republican nominees, respectively, for surveyor in Somerset County, have both declined to serve.

An exchange says Milford is the most populous and the wickedest peninsular town south of Wilmington, but the Presbyterian, Episcopal and Baptist churches there are all without ministers.

A boy pointed a loaded gun at a little girl at Somerset, Md. and threatened to shoot. "All right," she said, confidently; "it couldn't hurt me, because ma says if I'm a good girl, nothing can hurt me." The boy pulled the trigger and the girl was killed.

Some heathen are not as much of the heathen as we think; read a Mahometan proverb, "God has bestowed the good things of this world to relieve our necessities, not to reward our virtues; these will be rewarded in another world." We know of no greater necessity to be relieved than a stubborn cold, and we know of no better relief than Dr. Bull's Cough Syrup.

Mr. A. J. Lawler, 172 S. Broadway, Baltimore, Md., says: "Malaria and dyspepsia troubled me for nine years. Brown's Iron Bitters gave me relief."

Are you disturbed at night and broken of your rest by a sick child suffering and crying with pain of cutting teeth? If so, send at once and get a bottle of MRS. WINSLOW'S SOOTHING SYRUP FOR CHILDREN TEETHING. It will relieve the poor little sufferer immediately. Depend upon it, mothers, there is no mistake about it. It cures dysentery and diarrhea, regulates the stomach and bowels, cures wind colic, softens the gums, reduces inflammation and gives tone and energy to the system. MRS WINSLOW'S SOOTHING SYRUP FOR CHILDREN TEETHING is pleasant to the taste and is the prescription of one of the oldest and best female physicians and nurses in the United States, and is for sale by all druggists throughout the world. Price 25 cents.

All the ministers of Berlin have signed a declaration that hereafter they will refuse to marry any person who has been divorced.

The town commissioners of Ridgely have passed an ordinance providing for the arrest and punishment of tramps and vagrants.

The employees of the Diamond State Telephone Company and Wm. Roach, Milford, were in a squabble over the location of a pole in front of Roach's residence last Saturday. Roach placed himself in the hole where the pole was to be located. A lawsuit followed.

At some of our seashore resorts, seawater is used as a medicinal beverage, mostly to reduce obesity. It is brought in by fishermen from far out, to be safe from any pollution. Three glasses daily is the usual dose.

During last May an infant child of our neighborhood was suffering from cholera infantum. The doctors had given up all hopes of recovery. I took a bottle of Chamberlain's Colic, Cholera and Diarrhea Remedy to the house, telling them I felt sure it would do good if used according to directions. In two days time the child had fully recovered. The child is now vigorous and healthy. I have recommended this remedy frequently and have never known it to fail. —Mrs. Curtis Baker. For sale by Hugh Duffey, Hillsboro; R. J. Colston, Denton.

Look out that your nurses do not drug your little ones with laudanum, paregoric or other soothing remedies. Give them Dr. Bull's Baby Syrup, which innocent remedy is warranted not to contain opiates.

Denton has a town law prohibiting horses to run at large on the streets. We hope it will be enforced.

Sheriff Griffin of Talbot County challenges anybody in Easton to play croquet for the championship of the town.

Ross, the colored man who was shot at a Bush Meeting some

time since in Centreville and who was reported dead, is still alive and has been in court as a witness against the parties accused of shooting him.

Near Hillsborough, a gentleman by the name of Barcus had in his employ a native of Poland and his wife, and also a German boy. We learn on Sunday, the boy took down a pistol from its usual place, saying that he intended to show them how they shot rabbits in his country. It is supposed that the boy did not know the pistol was loaded. He pulled the trigger and the load passed just under the arm of the lady of the house into the body of the Pole's wife. She died in a short time. The husband became almost frantic, but the family did not apprehend further trouble than the grief it was natural for the terrible disaster to occasion. In a short time after the death of the wife, however, someone on the farm had occasion to go to the barn, when they found the disconsolate man hanging by the neck, also dead. His troubles were more than he could bear.

At a distillery near Bridgeville a colored boy inserted a siphon in a barrel of apple brandy and drank until he fell to the ground unconscious. He will probably die. The brandy continued to run after he fell, and 40 gallons, valued at $150, were wasted.

Jacob Johensen, near Vienna, had a very narrow escape during a recent storm. A bolt of lightning, after striking the house, passed on to the room where Mr. Johensen was sleeping, tore the bedstead to pieces, throwing him across the room without injuring him in the least.

A vendor of rattlesnake oil did a land office business with the deputies at the jail Monday night, said one observer about the jail. He turned up Monday with a rattlesnake around his neck and loudly proclaimed the virtues of the oil as an antidote for mosquito bites whenever he could get a knot of men to turn their attention for a moment from the scenes and incidents of the trial. The mosquitoes from the Choptank marshes were the only attackers at the jail, and the deputies rubbed rattlesnake oil vigorously on their exposed faces and hands.

Joseph Paul, a farmer near Federalsburg, was seriously injured a few days ago when his large peach wagon, containing himself and about twenty-five Bohemian women and children was upset at Secretary. Paul drove to Secretary to get the Bohemian laborers to work in canneries near this town. While they were getting on his wagon, a runaway team crashed into it, turning the wagon over and catching the occupants beneath. Mr. Paul received a gash three inches long across his face and suffered internal injuries, but excepting minor injuries all the children escaped.

P. E. Corkran is contemplating the purchase of a twenty passenger automobile truck, with which he will meet all trains and boats, run excursion parties, etc. The machine is said to be worth $3,500.

"What shall we do to entertain our girls?" says a religious exchange. A man who needs advice as to how to entertain his girls is not fit to edit a religious paper. We suggest that he should take one of them out buggy riding in the afternoon, tell her what a daisy she is and how insipid and fixed up that other girl is. Then he should take the other girl out for ice cream after supper and tell her confidentially how very uninteresting and awkward the buggy-riding girl is. When the two girls meet, the religious editor can depend on them entertaining each other without his personal assistance.

President Elliott of Harvard College affirms that "there is a fundamental pervading difference between all men and all women, which extends to their minds as much as to their bodies." Professor Agassiz adds that they need a different diet.

An Indianapolis parent has been fined $6 for giving his minor son a glass of lager beer.

Seven Indians made a raid into Brown County, Texas, but were captured. After being washed, seven white men stood revealed. They were hung out to dry.

Judges Ingraham and Brady have decided in the General Term of the Supreme Court of New York that a man cannot recover damages for the death of his wife, even if willfully murdered, but he may sue for the value of her services and society while she is under the care of the doctor.

A man named Guy Carleton Haynes died in Boston, March 15th [1877], aged 101. He was the youngest of 23 children. His oldest sister, Mrs. Hannah Reddington, was more than 50 years his senior. She had grandchildren and great grandchildren older than he. Three of his brothers served in the French War in Canada 29 years before he was born.

In an old cathedral in the Netherlands, the monks exhibit a phial, which appears empty but is very dark. They tell the visitor that it is one of their most precious relics, for in it is preserved some of the darkness that Moses spread over the land of Egypt. —*posted between 1873 and 1915.*

Did you ever consider that the advent of paved roads may not have been viewed as an improvement by everyone?

DIRT ROADS NEEDED: We have heretofore referred to the manifest need of a dirt roadway alongside the state highways. A correspondent of the Baltimore Sun again brings up this matter, saying:

"The softer, yielding dirt road does not jar and stiffen up horses' limbs like the hard, solid stone or paved roadway, so careful teamsters would generally prefer the side dirt roads, while automobilists, preferring the center, would thus keep out of each other's way and lessen chances of accidents.

"A wider grading of the road would also give automobilists more room to handle and check up their machines if steering gears broke, tires burst or other things went wrong. This additional grading and smoothing, costing probably less than $100 per mile, would be worth many times that in added beauty, convenience, safety and wear-saving. So, by all means make smooth, graded dirt tracks border each side of all our oiled state roads." —*8/28/1915*

We take the roadside produce stand for granted today, and some of them are now housed in buildings that approach the size of a chain store, but when did the phenomenon begin?

THE LITTLE BOOTH ON THE FARM: One of the interesting developments or changes of method that has come with the motor car is the little booth which is set up on the farm close by the highway, from which automobilists are buying fruit and vegetables fresh from trees and vines. The system eliminates the middleman, but as a rule it does not eliminate his fee; for the producer usually quietly pockets this and the consumer, ultimately, as usual, is content in securing his foodstuffs fresh, even at the cost of going after them. The system is developing especially at the summer places where "cottagers" often seem to have little to do but to ride about the country in their cars. —9/4/1915

They don't make winters the way they used to.

THE MAROONED OF HOLLANDS ISLAND: Two hundred and fifty people on Hollands Island were for some time this week in danger of starvation. They were marooned by the great ice floes, and boats with provisions could not reach them.

The Baltimore News Wednesday said: The Revenue Cutter Apache, Capt. G. Creighton Carmine, won in the race to reach Hollands Island in the lower Chesapeake, where 300 people have been marooned for thirty-three days. According to wireless dispatches received by the News, she arrived at 8 o'clock Wednesday morning in sight of the little sand bar after battling with the ice for practically twenty-four hours. —2/10/1912

Ah, the wonders of modern technology:

THE LATEST INVENTION IN USEFUL HOUSEHOLD ARTICLES: Within the last few years there has been expended a great deal of inventive thought and genius upon what may properly be classed as household articles, the most noted results of which are the production of the sewing machine, the wringer, the washing machine, the carpet sweeper, &c. Almost every week we chronicle the advent of some new invention by which the cares and labors of housekeeping are lessened and woman's work made easier.

The newest thing to challenge our attention and gladden the heart of the housekeeper is what is called the Novelty Brush Holder, Carpet Stretcher and Sweeper, a very simple contrivance designed to firmly hold in position any kind of a brush or duster, having an extension handle that enables one to wash or dust windows, walls or ceilings without the aid of a stepladder. That is one of its conveniences, and it is also one of the best carpet sweepers in the market, holding the brush firmly at an angle. It cleans the carpet thoroughly, raises no dust and does not wear the carpet like the ordinary broom or brush, and will outwear half a dozen brooms. As a handle for the scrubbing brush it is the best device ever made, no more kneeling on the floor, no more backaches or sare [sic] fingers.

As a carpet stretcher alone it is worth its cost, as a carpet of any size can be laid evenly without any of the labor and vexation usually attending such work. It is strong, simple, thoroughly made, cannot get out of order, has no screws, lever or hinges, is compact, cheap and durable.

It is manufactured by Brown & Co., Cincinnati, the well-known manufacturers of useful household articles, and is sold only by their agents to housekeepers. The real utility of this article will at once be seen by those most interested, and we predict for it a large sale. Every housekeeper in the land will want one. Any reliable lady or gentleman wishing remunerative employment would do well to secure the agency for this county, which can be done by enclosing a stamp for descriptive circular and terms to Brown & Co. Grand Hotel Building, Cincinnati, O. —5/24/1879

And what ever became of:

THE BRADLEY PROMETHOR: This wonderful motor has at last been perfected and is now in successful operation in a large establishment in Philadelphia. The new system of power consists of a motive gas evolved from water by its mechanical atomization with the use of heat, and Mr. R. D. Bradley, who is a native of this county [Caroline], claims that this work is not only an invention but a discovery—not only a mechanism but a system of engineering. He is very enthusiastic over his invention and has various patent documents received from all over the world. —5/3/1879

Oh, my—the beginnings of tabloid journalism.

AN ENOCH ARDEN CASE: Some two or three years ago Mr. A. Leigniel, a Roman Catholic priest, tiring of the state of celibacy exacted by the Romish church, purchased property near the village of Preston in the lower part of this county. After taking possession, he began to cast around for a helpmeet [sic] in life, finally fixing his long-pent-up affections on one of Preston's charming daughters. All passed along pleasantly until in early December of last year, when Mr. L. suddenly became possessed of a desire to take a trip to Belgium for the very worthy purpose of seeing his parents. After making an extended trip through England and France, he suddenly returned Sunday last via the steamer Highland Light to find his wife the wife of another; for Mrs. Leigniel, no sooner finding herself without a protector, than she gave her heart and hand to another child of sorrow, and no doubt would have enjoyed herself hugely with her second alliance had not her former husband returned. As soon as Mr. L. heard of the whereabouts of his spouse, he proceeded to hunt her up. She saw him coming; ran to meet him; and overwhelmed with joy, fell weeping into his arms.

First love proving the stronger, she returned to the bed and board of her first love, where we draw the curtains and leave the scene. —4/14/1877

And this last clip is guaranteed to raise your curiosity...

IN JAIL: The friends of J. E. Johnson brought a lot of his goods and chattels to our town and placed them in jail on Thursday last. Mr. Johnson's friends decided on the 4th of November last that he should make the jail his home for the next two years, and his furniture has been placed there for his comfort and ease. Sheriff Evitts gave him the keys and has moved out of town. —12/13/1873

...unless you know that James E. Johnson was elected sheriff in 1873, and sheriffs used to live in the jail.

The Search
for Patty Cannon

In 1841, twelve years after Patty Cannon died in Delaware's Georgetown Jail, a twenty-three-page pamphlet—the *Narrative and Confessions of Lucretia P. Cannon, the Female Murderer*—was published in New York by Clinton Jackson and Erastus E. Barclay, two names that cannot be identified in any contemporary records, not even on the census rolls of five adjoining states.

Although this Gothic horror tale continues to provide the basis for numerous annual magazine and newspaper articles about Patty Cannon and the lawless assortment of kidnappers and murderers that operated along the Maryland-Delaware border in the first quarter of the nineteenth century, its pages contain little more than a few hints of truth.

It appears from records that Patty's given name was Martha, not Lucretia, and Jesse Cannon was her husband. In the *Narrative*, Patty's spouse is called Alonzo, and it is plausible that both names were selected by the author for the purpose of forging a mental connection to Lucretia Borgia (1480-1519), the daughter, by a mistress, of Cardinal Rodrigo Borgia, who later became Pope Alexander VI.

While my copy of *Encyclopedia Britannica* has nothing sinister to say about Lucrezia Borgia's personality or conduct, there are many legends that suggest she was guilty of notorious behavior, including incest and murder. In the genre of fiction, Lucrezia and Patty may, indeed, have much in common.

The *Narrative* informs us that L. P. Hanly, the liberally educated son of a wealthy nobleman, married a woman of intrigue, who was believed by some to be a witch. When Hanly's father disowned his offspring for intemperance and lack of prudence, the young man and his bride set sail for Canada.

In Montreal and later at St. Johns, the couple raised four daughters and a son, we are told, but Hanly gravitated into the business of smuggling and eventually killed a man by splitting his skull with an axe, then stabbing him in the heart and cutting his throat. He was apprehended by authorities and hanged for his crime.

To support her large family, Mrs. Hanly opened what the *Narrative* refers to as a "house of entertainment for persons traveling for pleasure."

Lucretia Hanly was sixteen when Alonzo Cannon, identified as a "respectable wheelwright" from lower Delaware and "possessed of considerable money," happened to stop at the inn for a few days. He fell ill and Lucretia nursed him back to health, winning his affections in the process. They were wed, the story goes, and Alonzo returned to Delaware with his bride, where the couple established Cannon's Ferry on the Nanticoke River.

Historical documents, however, inform us that Cannon's Ferry was in operation at least as early as 1765, when Patty and Jesse could have been no more than very young children, and almost certainly before that date. Isaac and Jacob Cannon, along with their mother, Elizabeth, owned and operated the ferry from 1780 until the brothers died, a month apart, in 1843. They were distant cousins to Jesse, who was never part of the ferry enterprise.

Many other verifiable facts stand in dispute of the *Narrative*, and I won't even speculate on the odds that a wheelwright (or carpenter, as Jesse appears to have actually been) from then remote and undeveloped Sussex County, Delaware, might have been sightseeing in Canada shortly after the American Revolution.

Writers of fiction have been Patty's primary biographers in the nearly two centuries since her death, and no one appears to have conducted even a cursory search for her origins beyond quoting the *Narrative*. I have asked dozens of Delmarva natives where Patty Cannon was born, and from those who have an opinion, the consistent answer is "Canada."

George Alfred Townsend, in his acclaimed historical novel (and please place emphasis on the word "novel") *The Entailed Hat* (1884), has Patty make the following statement about her roots in a discussion with the fictional character Colonel McLane: "I've hearn my grandfather was a lord. A gypsy woman enticed his son and he married her. His father drove him from his door, an' his wife fetched him on her money to Canady, where she went into the smugglin' business at St. John's, half-way between Montreal and the United States."

"And he was hanged there for assassinating a friend who detected him?"

"They says so, honey. Anyhow, he was hanged. We gals was beautiful. Says mother: 'It's a hard world, but don't let it beat you, gals. Marry if you kin. Anyway, you must live, and you can't live off of women.' I married a Delaware man, and so I quit bein' Martha Hanley and became Patty Cannon."

At this point in his story, Townsend refers the reader to a footnote: "The origin of Patty Cannon is in doubt; a pamphlet published near her time [the *Narrative and Confessions*] gives it as above, with strong circumstantial embellishments, yet there are neighbors who say she was of Delaware and Maryland stock—a Baker and a Moore. The weight of tradition is the other way."

Surely, when Patty and Jesse lived on the Maryland-Delaware border at present day Reliance, her neighbors knew exactly who she was; there was simply no compelling reason to pass that information along. No one wrote it down, and so it was lost to history. Researchers who have attempted to pursue the Baker and Moore suggestion have thus far found only dead ends.

Octogenarian and still practicing attorney Bernard John Medairy, Jr. has been fascinated with the story of Patty Cannon for years and has rooted out many unpublished documents related to members of the gang and their activities. He believes he knows who Patty Cannon was, and while he has not provided me with conclusive proof of her pedigree, many will consider the circumstantial evidence to be compelling. Bear with me, now, while I seem to stray from the subject for a few minutes.

Before the turn of the eighteenth century, Hugh Handley had acquired several tracts of land in Dorchester County, Maryland. One of those was Handley's Regulation, a parcel of five hundred and fifty acres situated along the Chicamacomico River that was later deeded to his son, also named Hugh, who raised three children there: Handy, Levin and Mary.

There is little to document the detailed lives of the Handleys, though it is clear they held a prominent position in the community. Both Handy and Levin benefited from a liberal education and were appointed by the Dorchester Court to oversee construction of two roads in the county.

But the brothers apparently had little else in common. While Handy continued the traditional business of the family plantation, Medairy claims that Levin developed a passion for horses and an unbridled social life.

Horseracing in Maryland was then a popular distraction for people of all classes. It attracted large crowds, and celebrations and parties followed the races, sometimes continuing for days. One popular track was located at New Market (now East New Market), only a few miles from Handley's Regulation, and it was here that Levin raced his favorite stallion, Masron. Some believe that Patty Cannon and Joe Johnson, Patty's son-in-law and perhaps the most violent member of the Cannon Gang, may also have raced horses at the New Market track.

During the Revolution, the Handley brothers were appointed to positions of leadership in the Dorchester Militia. Handy's commission was granted on the advisement of the chairman of the Committee of Observation, a group of prominent citizens who deliberated on matters relative to public and political welfare. Governor Thomas Johnson, himself a thoroughbred racing enthusiast, appointed Levin a captain in the Upper Battalion of the Dorchester Militia without the usual recommendation.

Field officers from Dorchester were incensed at Levin's assignment to their ranks, and after conducting a court of inquiry in Cambridge on June 11, 1778 to examine Levin's moral character, Lt. John Goldsborough wrote: "The Said Court are of Opinion that the Said Handley ought not to enjoy a Commission—and do request the Lieutenant of this County to represent this as our Opinion to his Excellency the Governor and Council."

On June 13, Colonel Henry Hooper, commander of military operations on the lower Eastern Shore, penned the following to Governor Johnson: "I must beg your Excellency's permission to lay before you in council a report made to me from the Field Officers of this County, respecting Capt. Levin Handley, a Militia Officer, whose character, if I am permitted to give you my opinion, I think too infamous for his continuance in office. Capts. Smoot and Daffin can, I believe, give full satisfaction to his general character."

Johnson ignored the memo.

In September, 1779 the Dorchester County Grand Jury handed down two indictments against Levin Handley, one for stealing five barrels of Indian corn from James Mowbray and another for forcibly taking a cow from the same plantation, but Tories and British barges were plundering the peninsula at the time and militiamen were busy. No warrant was ever issued for Handley's arrest.

On December 16, 1779 the following notation was entered on Dorchester County Militia records: "Capt. Levin Handley ran away."

During the following year, Handley stole a slave named Abe from Powell Cox in Dorchester County, and on New Year's Day, 1781 he stole another slave, Ben, from William Dawson in Talbot County.

Indictments were again drawn, and Judge Nicholas Thomas of the General Court of the Eastern Shore issued a warrant for Levin's arrest. The accused was taken into custody by High Sheriff John Stevens of Dorchester County and confined in irons in the Cambridge Jail.

Gustavus Scott, a former member of the Continental Congress and one of Maryland's ablest legal advocates, was retained by Handley for his defense. To pay Scott's legal fees, Handley sold him the

49

stallion Masron for seventy pounds.

The prosecution was conducted by Maryland's Attorney General, Luther Martin, whom historian Henry Adams once called "the most formidable of American advocates." Martin served as Maryland's chief prosecutor for thirty years and also gained fame as a defense attorney in such cases as the treason trial of Aaron Burr.

Proceedings against Handley for stealing William Dawson's slave began in the General Court of the Eastern Shore in the Talbot County Courthouse on April 26, 1781. The theft of a slave was classified as a felony, a crime then punishable by death. After considering the testimony, an all male jury from Dorchester, Talbot, Queen Anne's, Caroline and Kent Counties returned a verdict of guilty.

Scott's appeal on behalf of Handley was heard by Judge Thomas on September 13, when Thomas concluded: "The defendant said no more than what at first he had said," and then pronounced: "It is considered by the Court here, that Levin Handley be taken back to the Prison of Dorchester County, and from thence be drawn to the place of execution, and there be hanged by the neck, until he is dead."

At this point, Handley's only hope lay in a pardon from the governor of Maryland, but his friend Thomas Johnson had been replaced by Thomas Sims Lee, a colonel in the Prince George's County Militia and a strict disciplinarian. Lee reviewed Handley's petition and accompanying letters requesting a pardon, then promptly responded by signing a warrant for the prisoner's execution.

Levin's son Handy, according to Medairy, then the youngest to bear that traditional family name, was lying in a Virginia hospital at 11:00 a.m. on November 7, 1781, when his father was loaded on a cart and driven to his execution. Apparently embarrassed by his parent's arrest, Handy had joined the Third Regiment of the Maryland Line, and several days before Cornwallis surrendered the British forces under his command on the Yorktown Peninsula, effectively ending the Revolutionary War, an artillery shell had shattered his left leg.

Among those who did visit Handley in his cell on the morning of November 7, Medairy believes, was a sixteen-year-old daughter named Martha, known to family and friends as "Patty."

Handy Handley, whom Medairy contends was Levin's son and Patty's brother, recovered from his wounds and returned to Dorchester County, where he married Nicey Hooper, a widow several years his senior, whose maiden name had been Cannon and who was the aunt of Jesse Cannon, the man who would later become the husband of Martha "Patty" Cannon.

Both Medairy and Townsend's novel claim that Elizabeth Handley (Townsend spells it "Hanley") was Patty's youngest sister, and that she was raised by Ebenezer Johnson, known as the "pirate of Broad Creek," at his home on that Nanticoke tributary. Ebenezer's son Joe married Patty's daughter, and his daughter, Brittania, became the wife of Patty's son.

Elizabeth Handley, records show, was betrothed to a man by the name of Bartholomew Twiford, who owned a plantation and wharf on the Nanticoke River, a mile downstream from the mouth of Broad Creek and just below the Maryland-Delaware line. Tradition agrees with Medairy and Townsend that Betty Twiford was Patty Cannon's sister, and the house that stood on the property until recent years is still referred to as "Patty Cannon's house" by a few of the older area residents. Captain Ebenezer Johnson, tradition also claims, was shot to death in the Twiford house while defending Betty's interests against intruders.

We know that early census enumerators rode on horseback or in a carriage from house to house, recording statistics as they went. The census, therefore, is a fairly reliable resource when it comes to identifying one's neighbors.

Something that Medairy had not discovered but which adds a measure of credence to his conclusion is that Sally Handley appears on the 1790 Census for Dorchester County as a neighbor of the Wrights and Wilsons who lived at Wilson's Cross Roads, later renamed Johnson's Cross Roads and eventually Reliance—where Jesse Cannon also lived.

While I have no proof that Sally was Levin's widow, some researchers believe she was, and it is not unreasonable to surmise that Sally may have moved to Wilson's Cross Roads after her husband's death to be near relatives. She had no claim to the Handley property on the Chicamacomico River, only fourteen miles distant as the crow flies.

Medairy reports that Levin Handley fathered eight children, though he cannot refer me to a document listing them by name. In Sally Handley's household in 1790, there was one male over the age of sixteen and five females. If only the census takers had been required to list the names of everyone living in a household.

So what cards do we now hold in the game to conclusively identify Patty Cannon?

For one hundred and sixty-two years, nearly everyone has accepted as factual a bizarre novelette that can now be disproved in almost every detail—a legend that claims Patty's father was L. Hanly and that he was hanged in Canada. But there are hints of truth in the *Narrative*, and one of them is the use of names that are similar to those of actual people.

Is it only a coincidence, then, that a man by the name of Levin Handley, of the correct age to have been Patty's father, was hanged not in Canada but in Cambridge, Maryland, twenty miles from what would become the operational center of the Cannon-Johnson Gang?

Then we have Handy Handley, claimed to be the son of Levin, who married Jesse Cannon's aunt, a fact that certainly established a relationship between the Handleys of Chicamacomico and the Cannons living in the vicinity of Wilson's Cross Roads. That Handy and Nicey married is a matter of record.

And there is the marriage and tradition of Betty Handley and the possibility that Levin's family moved to Wilson's Cross Roads after his execution, which would have made them neighbors to Jesse Cannon, Patty's husband to be.

What we do not seem to have is documentation that Sally Handley was Levin's wife and, most important of all, a certified list of the names of Levin's children. The search goes on.

Grandpa Hurley
And the Tax Police

It occurred to me the other day that I hadn't stopped to see Grandpa Hurley in a coon's age, and that reminded me of how a couple of swigs from Grandpa's old stoneware jug can turn a lazy afternoon into one of pure delight.

When I pulled off on the oyster-shell pad next to Colonel duPont's former duck hunting shack on Clam Creek, I was surprised to find the porch empty. There hasn't been a fit afternoon since Grandma departed for that better land that Grandpa hasn't held court there from his old blue rocker. But what really sent a chill up my spine was the vacant spot next to the chair, where Grandpa always parks his gallon jug with the blue bird on one side.

Grandpa is not a young man, and a couple of months ago he decided it was time to begin preparations for his own hereafter. I told him that having thoughts about dying has been known to set dormant fates in motion, and he might better apply his energies to more joyful tasks. But, like a spring marsh fire, once Grandpa takes a direction, there's not much anybody can do to sway him from it.

Cousin Job is Clam Snout's jack-of-all-trades—from accountant to carpenter to shoemaker to undertaker—and Grandpa commissioned him to cut a stone and set it next to Grandma's in the East Clam Snout Graveyard. It's a fine looking monument in the old style, chiseled from genuine Pennsylvania limestone to match Grandma's. So far, it reads:

Archibald Hurley
Born: October 13, 1911

You can't believe everything you read.

That epitaph has been Grandpa's mantra for as long as anybody can remember. He had Grandma embroider it on some pillowcases back in 1945, right after he came back from the big war, and he's laid his head on those words every night since.

He said the words just came to him one night while he lay sleepless in a snowy foxhole outside Bastone, during the Battle of the Bulge. "It was like the time the Ten Commandments come to Moses," Grandpa told me once. "It was just one of them spiritual things."

I guess you can't have your mental apparatus so close to a spiritual revelation for that many years and not have it become a part of you. I'm telling you all of this because it's connected to the reason I didn't find Grandpa on his blue rocker on the porch as I had expected.

When my knock on the shack door went unanswered, I drove on over to Clam Snout and stopped at Chris Wiley's Barbershop, Hardware, Fish and Produce Market, Family Restaurant, Bar, Fur Dealership and Ferry. Chris hasn't taken the ferry sign down, even though the state finally decided to fix the old bridge.

Due to Clam Snout's outspoken, anti-Annapolis politics during the years when Willie Don Schaefer was governor, it appeared for a while as though the island community was going to revert to the isolation of its first two hundred years. That's when Chris tacked a new plank to the end of his much-expanded signboard. "Ferryin' runs deep in Willey blood," Chris proudly told me at the time. The now sixth-generation family business got its start with a hand-drawn cable scow that his great, great, great, great-grandfather won in a game of "58" from Captain Horatio Gray in 1799.

Chris' parking lot was jammed with a couple of pickups and Grover Cleveland Gray's golf cart. Grover believes that electric cars are the wave of the future, and he doesn't intend to be tied up in some backwater gut when the wave breaks. Actually, the golf cart was left there a month ago, when it ran out of juice while Grover was getting a haircut and the batteries wouldn't take a charge anymore. I was pleased to find Grandpa's '68 Chevy sitting next to it.

With all parking slots occupied, I had to block the lane to Captain John's crab shack, which doubles as town hall. Captain John gave up crabbing ten years ago, and there hasn't been a town meeting in almost as long, so I had little concern that I would inconvenience anyone.

As I wrestled open the weathered, pine-plank door, I could see immediately that there were new doings at the island's premier place of business; T-shirts were hanging everywhere. "What's not to like about a horseshoe crab" was the first one to grab my attention.

I stepped aside and held the portal for Lulu Mae Insley, who rushed by me with a two-handed death grip on a carryout box full of Mrs. Paul's fish sticks and a "Thank you kindly."

"Chris is into horseshoe crabs now?" I blurted, not really expecting a reply.

"They's left over from the festival," Lulu Mae offered over her shoulder.

"What festival?" I called after her as she dashed across the road in the direction of her pink and blue ten-wide, but my informant had already disappeared behind the trailer. Lulu Mae's husband, Ike, is not a patient man, even when he's sober, and she's careful not to irritate him, especially when he's hungry.

I found the crowd assembled in the bar. Thomas Jefferson Abbott and Bubba Gray were silently hunkered over two mugs of Dogfish tap, and Grandpa and Chris were gathered around a pile of T-shirts at a table in the corner.

"What's going on around here?" I interrupted the silence. "T-shirts and festivals?"

"Where you been, Junior?" Grandpa squinted at me over his wire-rimmed specs.

55

"I guess it has been a while," I admitted. "So tell me about all these T-shirts?"

"It jest come to me," Grandpa growled. "Jest like that time when the Jerries had us pinned down at Bastone."

And what's that, Grandpa?"

"That it's time I share it out."

"You're gonna have to give me a boost here, Grandpa; I'm not in the boat with you yet."

"Jest like it come to me in that foxhole, it come to me in the shack one night when I was havin' too much hip pain to sleep—that it would be a worthwhile thing to share it out with other folks."

"Share what? Grandpa.

"You can't believe ever'thin' you read."

"O.K., I'll buy that."

"I was tellin' Chris here 'bout how it would be a missionary sort of thing to let people know they jest can't believe ever'thin' they read. He said he seen over to the beach where they was sellin' all kinds of T-shirts with all kinds of advice printed on 'em, and people was jest bustin' their knuckles a-reachin' fur their wallets to buy 'em. Chris says, 'Maybe you oughta put that sayin' on a T-shirt. Thataway, you kin git people to pay fur the shirt, and then they spreads the word around fur free.'

"So I says, 'Whar you s'pose they gits all them T-shirts from?'

"Chris recollected he seen some over to Cambridge Copy Shop when he went to git his new menu printed up fur the restaurant. So I had Cousin Job carry me over there, and I talked to the man. He fixed me right up. He wrote 'You can't believe ever'thin' you read' on half a dozen T-shirts—one small, two mediums, two large and one extra large—in day-glo pink.

"Chris hanged one up in the window and another'n over the bar, and we done real good—sold three of 'em to some boys that come down here crabbin' one afternoon from over there to State College. Weren't 'nough crabs runnin' to cover the bottom of the basket, so they was settin' 'round the bar. After a couple Dogfish draughts, they got to snickerin' over the T-shirt, and one boy says, 'Let's buy some and wear 'em to Professor So-And-So's class tomorrow.'

"I told Chris: 'Now, you see, that's what a education will do fur you. They know the good word when they see it, and they're gonna share it out to others.'

"Right after that, I was sayin' to Chris if he thought I oughta git another half dozen shirts printed up, and some salesman from the city happened at the bar. He pulls me aside and tells me I could save a lot of money to have 'em done up in Honduras or China and some other place I ain't never heard of. I told him: 'Look here, young fella, you got your boots on the wrong feet. If'n them places is futher'n Cambridge, it don't make one bit of sense in this world to even think about it.'

"Day after that, Chris was tellin' me how he read 'bout them horseshoe crabs—how they throws all the way back to dinosaur days, or someplace thereabouts, and how they're getting more 'n' more scarce ever' year. I told him, 'Why don't you start up a horseshoe crab festival right here in Clam Snout. Y'all been lookin' fur some turn to bring them tourist folk 'round town.'

"Chris says, 'How kin I do that when they ain't been neither horseshoe crab in Clam Bay in a hunnert year, if'n there ever was one then.'

"I says, 'They ain't no shad in the river, neither ways, but that don't stop nobody from havin' a big time to the Shad Festival up there in Vianna ever' year.'

"Well, he couldn't hardly argue with all that knowledge, and that's how the First Annual Clam Snout Horseshoe Crab Festival come about. You shouldn't not have missed it, Junior.

"Tommy Horton wrote somethin' up fur the *Daily Blunder*, 'n' Cap'n John's wife, Brenda—she took one of them correspondence courses in art one time, you know—she made up a sign to put up there on Route 50, showin' directions how to git here.

"Well, ever'body jumped right on the wagon. Town council got some shirts made up with a horseshoe crab on the back what Brenda drawed, and up front it says: "What's not to like about a horseshoe crab.' Emma Sue made up a bunch: 'Emma Sue's Craft Shop—Only chicken-neckers shop at St. Michaels.' And a writer fella from up to Vianna come down to sell his books, and he had a shirt on what said, 'I've been to Puckum?' Couldn't figger that one out no ways. Ever'body knows you can't never get to Puckum."

Chris sorted through the rumpled pile of shirts on the table, pulled out one in black with multi-colored lettering and held it up for me to read: "Willey's Barbershop, Hardware, Fish and Produce Market, Family Restaurant, Bar, Fur Dealership and Ferry—If we ain't got it, you don't need it!"

"We kept that man over to the Copy Shop right busy fur a time," Chris offered.

"So how come you've got so many shirts left over?" I asked. "Didn't anybody show up for the festival?"

"Humph!" Grandpa snorted. "Must of had twenty cars parked all over the place when it come ten o'clock, and then this fella shows up in a brown suit, and he had one of them city hats on, and he had a state trooper with him. He come by ever'body's table and said, 'Whar's your tax license?'

"Ever'body didn't know what in the world the man was preachin' at. I says, 'What tax license you talkin' 'bout? Ever'body 'round here done paid our taxes back in April.'

"Man says, 'If you wanna sell somethin', you gotta have a State of Maryland tax license and collect taxes fur Com'troller Willie Don Schaefer,' and then he declared the festival shut down.

"I told him: 'It's a sorry thing we never follered up on joinin' the State of Delaware back before the bridge, and don't think you heard the last of that, neither.'

"Git me a license to sell T-shirts—and put a tax on 'em. The man ain't nothin' but a crazy, chicken-necker! Next thing, them 'Nap'lis boys'll 'spect me to git a license to drive my Chevy down here to set a spell with Chris. When I see Addie Eckhart and Rick Coulbourne, I'm tellin' them political folks to have that daggone bridge took out, so them dadburned furriners 'crost the bay kin git back to mindin' their own business.

"Here, Junior, I'm gonna give you one of these here shirts so you kin remember that you just can't believe ever'thin' you read. You spread the word around, now, you hear. That's a worthwhile thing fur a body to think on."

58

It's like my late friend Mr. Flat always said, "People down to Clam Snout don't have much education, and they've never been anyplace else but there, but they've got a whole lot of wisdom."

Editor's Note: In spite of the best efforts of Hal Roth's two cats, Moppy and Cokie, he sometimes forgets to take his medication. The preceding story was written on one of those days.

Cypress Knees along the Pocomoke River

On a River
Out of Time

"It's the deepest river in the United States," I've been told a dozen times by Eastern Shore natives, and I've read the same claim nearly as often. One elderly gentleman went so far as to earnestly credit Delmarva's Pocomoke River with being the "deepest river in the world."

Charles C. Kensey, born a block from the Pocomoke in Snow Hill in 1884, comes a little closer to the truth in his privately published memoir, *The Pocomoke River* (1967). "The river is noted for its depth. It is said to be the deepest river in the United States for its width."

While an officer with the United States Corps of Engineers, to whom I spoke, would not guarantee even the latter claim, no one denies that the Pocomoke's winding, seventy-mile course, which begins its run in Delaware's Cypress Swamp and ends in Pocomoke Sound, is as wild and beautiful as any river in the region, and far more so than most. With a margin consisting primarily of swamp, there is no easy way to approach the water from land or to leave it, except at an occasional landing or crossing.

Stained by tannin and, some say, by iron deposits in its bordering bogs, the fresh waters of the river are tinted a shade of brown. Pocomoke means "dark waters" in the language of Native Americans who lived along its shores.

For me, the best choice to cruise this river out of time is on a lazy, Indian summer day after tinted leaves have begun to fall and cypress "hair" to shed. (Among our ancient conifers, the bald cypress is a rare, deciduous sibling.) On weekdays in autumn, one can drift silently for long periods through the Pocomoke's serene, almost prehistoric waterscape, shedding cares like spent foliage and almost believing the world is yours alone.

October 30 was as near to a perfect day as one is likely to experience—sunny and warm and with a light breeze out of the southwest. I launched my sixteen-foot runabout at Byrd Park in Snow Hill. The only boat I would see for the remainder of the day (until my rescue) was slowly working its way around Goat Island while the skipper and his wife cast artificial lures toward the shoreline and retrieved them with little twitches in the hope of enticing the strike of a bass. A young man fishing from shore at the boat ramp proudly announced that he had landed two.

My intentions were to make a quick run to Chesapeake Bay, then retreat at a leisurely pace, exploring and photographing points of interest. But the mystical morning light turned every bold cypress and river bend into a masterwork of art, and each new angle and spectacle compelled my hand to withdraw the throttle. By the time I reached Pocomoke City, I had taken more than a hundred photographs.

Among the captured images are river panoramas as well as individual trees in their settings. The buttressed trunks of cypress and their knees that rise from the dark, caressing waters are irresistible to me. I discovered one giant bearing the deep, spiraling scar of a recent lightning strike. The season had already browned its fronds, but now it will not green again with the awakening breath of spring.

I took several shots of an abandoned house, staring blankly at the river through a narrow passage in the trees—more of a cottage nestled in pines. But the attraction that most delayed my run stands on a low bluff, a short distance below Milbourne Landing and less than a hundred yards from the Pocomoke's northwest shore.

In his architectural history of Worcester County, Maryland—*Along the Seaboard Side* (1994)—Paul Baker Touart calls Cellar House "...one of Worcester County's best-built mid-eighteenth century dwellings" and refers to its exemplary Georgian woodwork as "some of the best of its kind on the lower Eastern Shore." It is the only remaining large-scale period house in the county that has brick gable ends and frame walls in front and back.

Scattered among the acres that surround this colonial gem is an assortment of metal sculptures: a silver archer turning slowly with the breeze, his bow drawn; a pink pig on the shore; a winged dragon "flying" among the limbs of cypress trees at the water's edge; and a wonderful assortment of other creatures, some might say "from Mars." And there is a story of two tragic deaths—a drowning and a murder—and ghosts; but those tales I shall save for another day.

Sometime around two o'clock, after photographing more cypress knees below Pocomoke City, I decided it was time to open the throttle and hold it there until I reached my planned destination.

There are no sounds more pleasant and soothing to me than those produced by nature, but the high-pitched whine of an outboard engine can convey its own special joy, and sudden silence can sometimes be traumatic. As my Aquasport Striper planed gracefully around a bend in the river at thirty-five knots, the engine suddenly quit. There was no sputter or cough of warning; it simply stopped, leaving me dead in the water.

From a clump of cypress knees twenty yards distant, a pair of nervous mallards lifted with a muffled splash and quickly disappeared around the bend on whistling wings, but the event failed to evoke my usual attentive smile. Instead, I turned from the bow toward the stern, and my heart sank a little when I failed to identify a landing in either direction.

The ebb tide was still retreating at a slow pace and I drifted with it while cramming my bulk between the seat and console to examine the electrical connections. I have no idea how any of it works, but I found nothing obviously loose or disconnected. Then I removed the cover from the engine, and that presented an even greater mystery. The fuel line seemed secure, and when I pumped the priming bulb, its resistance indicated that gas should have been available to the carburetor. There was nothing else that I knew how to do.

After half a dozen unsuccessful attempts to crank the engine back to life, I switched on my hand-held VHF radio to channel 16, depressed the call button and firmly spoke into the mike, "Calling DNR or Coast Guard on the Pocomoke River. Over."

Silence.

I figured the odds were not good for the Department of Natural Resources or the Coast Guard to have a boat on the river, but I repeated the call several times. I then dropped the Pocomoke qualification and invited a response from anyone connected to DNR or the Coast Guard.

Finally: "I'm stranded on the Pocomoke River below Pocomoke City and need assistance. If anyone can hear me, please respond. Over."

The silence was overwhelming.

I switched to one of the weather channels to be sure I had power and that the volume was properly set, then I pleaded again on other frequencies with the same results. So much for the reliability of portable VHFs in an emergency; their range is usually less than three miles.

I drifted quietly for a few minutes, considering my predicament. But when the almost stalled outgoing tide and a slight breeze from the opposite direction conspired to halt my progress, I took down one of the paddles I keep strapped below the gunwale and began to manually push the boat down river, where I could now see a house on a patch of high ground.

There are more constructive forms of exercise for guys over seventy with bad backs than propelling a couple of tons of fiberglass and steel and gas and gear with a canoe paddle, but I managed to reach the landing in about half an hour and secured the boat to a piling. There were several houses nearby, where I felt certain I could secure assistance—at least some information about where I might contact a mechanic or arrange a tow back to Pocomoke City.

On the assumption that it might suggest a boater in trouble as opposed to an axe murderer just emerged from the swamps with mayhem in mind, I unzipped my life jacket but did not remove it.

Several knocks on the closest house to the landing went unanswered, so I walked across the spacious yard to another. Two vehicles were parked in back and I could see a lighted chandelier through one window, but four knocks with long waits between brought no response. I walked around to the back. From inside the fence, a dog half-heartedly barked at me, and I stood for more long minutes, wooing the canine and waiting for someone to check on the commotion. No one did, at least not in any way that was visible to me. I moved on to the next residence, then across the road to a fourth with the same negative results at each.

What road was I on? I had no idea, but a short distance in one direction I could see a fifth house, and there was activity in the back yard. Limping from my leg brace and pain in my lower back, I hiked down the middle of the traffic-free blacktop.

A long driveway curved around the white rancher, joining the county road on either side. Behind the house, a car and a pickup were parked and a man was busying himself at a pair of sawhorses beside one of the outbuildings. With a friendly wave, I started up the lane toward him.

He quickly walked over to the pickup, which was facing me, and got in. I raised both hands, indicating that I wanted him to wait. In response, he started the engine and backed out of sight.

Hadn't he seen me? I continued up the driveway.

When I reached the rear of the house and the truck came into view again, the friendly fellow accelerated to the rear once more, out onto the road, and away he went. I stood dumbfounded in the middle of the driveway.

Well, maybe he hadn't seen me. There was still the other car, and the back door of the house was standing open inside the storm door. I walked over and knocked, not really expecting a response and got none.

Quitting the property in advance of what I considered might next be a shotgun blast, I walked to the intersection of another road to consider my plight.

After a few minutes, a car approached and I raised both arms in a "please stop" plea. The driver, a middle-aged man, waved and drove on. Several minutes later, another vehicle appeared from the opposite direction and I tried again to make the driver understand that I needed assistance. The young woman behind the wheel accelerated and ran the stop sign.

I reached in my pocket and extracted my cell phone. In most of the outback places I venture, I don't have a signal (Can you hear me now?), but this time it showed three bars. For the first time in my life, I dialed 911.

"Do you have an emergency?"

"I do not have a critical emergency, but I'm stranded and need help. May I explain my situation?"

The operator passed me on to Somerset County Central and they transferred me to the Department of Natural Resources, where I outlined my predicament in detail to a woman who listened patiently, then said, "I can't get any help to you for an hour."

"An hour will be fine; I have no other options."

I repeated the names on the two road signs at the intersection and told her I would wait there; then I sat down on the muddy bank next to a recently harvested cornfield.

About an hour later my phone rang. The DNR lady wanted to know where I was; her man couldn't find me.

"I'm sitting right next to the two road signs where I was when we first talked," and I gave her the names again.

"How close are you to the river?"

"A couple hundred yards."

"The officer in the Whaler didn't see you." (A "Whaler" is a boat.)

"Did you send a boat? I thought he was coming by car."

While a lot of chatter ensued between the lady and two other voices on her radio, an unmarked SUV pulled up, driven by a handsome young man wearing a camouflaged shirt and jeans. "Are you from DNR?" I asked as he rolled down the passenger side window.

He nodded.

I thanked the voice on the telephone and got in.

After telling my story to officer Jeff Howard and pointing out the location of my boat, he drove me to a nearby landing where Sergeant Scott Richardson was docked in an idling Whaler. Richardson, in turn, took me to my stranded boat, secured the bowline to his stern, and we slowly set off up river, the Whaler gracefully towing my considerably heavier vessel.

I suppose some might have been embarrassed, but I was too tired and hurting to be anything but grateful, and I relaxed and enjoyed the mellow glow that a soon-to-set sun splashed across the wild riverscape. And, of course, I took pictures all the way back to Pocomoke City, where Officer Howard met us at the community wharf in his SUV.

"Since all the budget cuts," Sergeant Richardson commented as we tied up, "we can't do many nice things like this for people anymore."

"Will I get a bill or do I pay my taxes next time without complaining?"

"The latter will do," Richardson smiled.

"Is there an outboard repair shop in town," I asked my rescuers.

"Ford's, but I don't know if he's still open. We'll run you over there."

Clyde Ford should have been home by then, relaxing after a long day in the shop, but he was working late to get a large boat off the street before dark. I thanked Officer Howard and Sergeant Richardson again, and their SUV turned the corner and disappeared into the dusk.

Mr. Ford agreed to look at my engine if I left it with him, but I explained that I still had a large problem: My van and trailer were fifteen miles away in Snow Hill, in a park that would soon close for the night. The mechanic graciously put aside his work and made several phone calls in an attempt to find me a ride, but no one was home. He then escorted me across the street to a lawn mower repair shop and explained my predicament.

"I'm not asking for a handout," I assured the owner; "I'm very willing to pay for transportation."

Several men were sitting inside the shop, talking. "I'll take you to Snow Hill," one of them called out, "if you don't mind riding in a jeep."

"I'll ride on your shoulders if I can get to Snow Hill," I told him, "and I intend to pay you."

"I won't take any money," Kenny Miles replied, and after driving me to Byrd Park, then leading me back in the dark to the Pocomoke City landing and helping to load the boat, he again refused my offer to pay. There are still some very good people left in the world.

I had informed a friend of my plans for the day and instructed her to call DNR if I failed to return by a reasonable hour, but I had not established the precise time to take such action. Before delivering the boat to Ford's and heading up the long road home. I took out my cell phone and made sure that the good people at DNR would not be bothered again.

Four days later, with a weekend in between, I received a call informing me that the engine had been repaired; my problem had been caused by a shorted electrical connection. After the drive back to Pocomoke City and an enjoyable chat with Clyde Ford, I wrote him a check and offered my driver's license for inspection. "Would you like to see a picture of me?" I asked.

"Nah," he said, "The only people who ever wrote me bad checks are people I know."

Sgt. Richardson Towing the Author to Pocomoke City

The Monument to Lydia Clark

Nau-Gwa-Ok-Wa

Her Indian name was Nau-Gwa-Ok-Wa (there is no English translation of its meaning), and to the day of her death she is said to have shunned the dress of white women, wearing only the cap and short skirt of her ancestors. She is believed to be the last of her people on Delmarva to speak the Nanticoke language. And though grandmother to a long line of chiefs, she is also remembered as the principal witness in a shameful 1855 trial in which the State of Delaware brought charges against storekeeper Levin Sockum for selling a quarter pound of gunpowder and a pound of shot to a neighbor. Her English name was Lydia Clark.

Delaware was a slave state in 1855 and, though free blacks outnumbered slaves in Sussex County, prejudice against African Americans was as deep-seated there as anywhere in the South. Blacks and mulattos, regardless of their status as individual citizens, were not permitted to vote, to sit on juries or to associate with whites in any public institution or function.

The denial of common civil rights to African Americans had been further advanced in many states after Nat Turner's slave rebellion in southeastern Virginia in 1831, and the fear of a similar uprising prompted the Delaware Legislature to pass a series of acts to more tightly control its black population.

71

Among the new restrictions, blacks were prohibited to assemble after 10:00 p.m. and were denied the right to own or use firearms. Delaware citizens guilty of "selling or loaning a firearm to any negro or mulatto," the law read, "shall be deemed guilty of a misdemeanor and shall be fined twenty dollars." Amendments in 1851 and 1852 tightened the restrictions to include ammunition.

Levin Sockum had been raised as a Nanticoke Indian, considered himself to be an Indian, and an existing photograph shows him to be Indian in appearance, but it is clear that forces were at work in 1855 to compel Indian descendants in Delaware to accept classification as Negroes.

Sockum's prominence and prosperity in the Indian River community made him an especially attractive target, and when he continued to proudly maintain his independence as an Indian, a suit was instituted in the Sussex County Court in Georgetown, charging him with selling ammunition to Isaac Harmon, whose name is recorded as Isaiah in the court records of the trial. Harman was Sockum's son-in-law. While indictment slips for 1855 are missing from the archives, it is verbal tradition in the community that Nathaniel Burton, one of Sockum's white neighbors, instituted the suit.

There was no question as to whether or not a sale had been made. Both Sockum and Harman freely admitted to the transaction. The legal issue was whether Harmon was an Indian, a Negro, a white or a mulatto. It was Burton's contention that Harmon was the latter.

Delaware's youthful new attorney general was George P. Fisher, and the Sockum trial was one of his first appearances in court. After Harmon and other witnesses called by Sockum's defense were unable to provide conclusive documentation of Harmon's racial heritage, Fisher called Lydia Clark to the stand. The prosecutor would later write the following statement of her and her testimony in a newspaper article.

"The proof of the sale of a quarter pound of powder and pound of shot to Harmon was given by Harmon himself; and in fact, admitted by Sockum's attorney. So the only fact I had to establish, in order to convict Sockum, was to identify Harmon as being a mulatto.... Lydia Clark, who swore that she was of blood kin to Harmon, was permitted to testify as to the traditions of the family in respect to their origin."

The charges become especially ludicrous when we weigh Fisher's next words.

"Harmon was a young man, apparently about five and twenty years of age, of perfect Caucasian features, dark chestnut brown hair, rosy cheeks and hazel eyes; and in making comparison of his complexion with others, I concluded that of all the men concerned in the trial he was the most perfect type of the pure Caucasian, and by odds the handsomest man in the court room.... The witness, Lydia Clark, his kinswoman, then 87 years old [her gravestone indicates she was in her seventies at the time], though only a half-breed, was almost as perfect a type of the Indian as I ever saw. She was as spry as a young girl in her movements, and of intelligence as bright as a new dollar; and this was substantially the genealogical tradition she gave of her family and that of Harmon.

"About fifteen or twenty years before the Revolutionary War, which she said broke out when she was a little girl some five or six years old, there was a lady of Irish birth living on a farm in Indian River Hundred, a few miles distant from Lewes, which she owned and carried on herself. Nobody appeared to know anything of her history or her antecedents. Her name she gave as Regua, and she was childless, but whether a maid or widow, or a wife astray, she never disclosed to anyone. She was much above the average woman of that day in stature, beauty and intelligence.

"The tradition described her as having a magnificent complexion, large, dark blue eyes and luxuriant hair of the most beautiful shade, usually called light auburn. After she had been living in Angola Neck quite a number of years, a slaver was driven into Lewes Creek, then a tolerable fair harbor, and was there, weather-bound, for several days. It was lawful then, for these were colonial times, to import slaves from Africa. Queen Elizabeth, to gratify her friend and favorite, Sir John Hawkins, had so made it lawful more than a century prior to this time.

"Miss or Mrs. Regua, having heard of the presence of the slaver in the harbor, and having lost one of her men slaves, went to Lewes, and to replace him, purchased another from the slave ship. She selected a very tall, shapely and muscular young fellow of dark gingerbread color, who claimed to be a prince or chief of one of the tribes of the Congo River, which had been overpowered in a war with a neighboring tribe and nearly all slain or made prisoners and sold into perpetual slavery. This young man had been living with his mistress but a few months when they were duly married and, as Lydia told the court and jury, they reared quite a large family of children, who as they grew up were not permitted to associate and intermarry with their neighbors of pure Caucasian blood, nor were they disposed to seek associations or alliance with the negro race; so that they were necessarily compelled to associate and intermarry with the remnant of the Nanticoke tribe of Indians...."

Fisher's newspaper article is the only written description of Lydia Clark's testimony, but a woman who attended the trial reported that a defense attorney attempted to confuse Lydia in his cross examination by asking: "Are you not Noke Norwood's brother?"

To which Lydia is said to have responded as quickly as the lash of a whip: "I would a bin if God almighty hadn't of made a mistake and made me a woman."

There are many legends among the so called Moors and Nanticokes of Delaware to explain their origin. One claims that a group of dark-skinned Spanish Moors established a colony in Delaware, and their present population has evolved through intermarriage between those colonists and the original Nanticokes.

The colonization legend is completely lacking in historical documentation, but there were Moors sold into slavery and brought to America with African slaves, and Spanish and Moorish seamen were also shipwrecked and set ashore in the Mid-Atlantic region.

The romantic legend that Lydia Clark told to the court has several versions in Delaware folklore. In one, a wealthy Spanish woman by the name of Raqua (Reegan in another tale) settled on a plantation near Indian River. She purchased a dark-skinned slave who spoke the Castilian tongue and married him when she discovered that he was actually a Spanish prince sold into slavery by treacherous relatives.

In yet another version, a beautiful, red-haired lady who lived on a plantation near Lewes is said to have lost her slaves when a mysterious plague swept the countryside. In the Lewes slave market she discovered a group of Moorish men and women on the block and purchased seven couples, the progeny of which later intermarried with Indian descendants of the region.

The most far-fetched belief I have encountered is that around 1000 B. C. an Egyptian princess, much to the displeasure of her father, fell in love with a young soldier. Though his stratagem may be difficult for us to understand, it is claimed that the father sent the soldier and his daughter on a voyage of exploration, accompanied by one of the king's priests.

The party eventually arrived in the New World and explored the St. Jones and Murderkill rivers in Delaware. Their craft having been damaged in route, a new vessel was constructed, but when it came time to return to the Mediterranean, the couple was abandoned. They managed to survive, the story claims, and they and their children are the ancestors of Delaware's present population of Moors and Nanticokes.

Some believe the Egyptian galley that is said to have brought the princess and her lover to America was uncovered nearly two hundred years ago in the muck of the St. Jones and that the rare lotus growing in the vicinity today originally sprang from seeds carried in its hull.

While Lydia Clark's testimony is considered to be little more than a fanciful tale that was concocted by her white benefactors, it was accepted by the court, and Isaac Harmon was subsequently declared to be a mixed descendant of white, African and Indian ancestors, thus biologically a mulatto. This meant that Levin Sockum was guilty as charged and was ordered to pay a fine of $20 and all costs of the trial. An appeal by his attorneys was denied.

Sockum was then charged with owning a firearm and did not deny the allegation. Indians were permitted to own firearms and most of them did. Lydia Clark was again called to the stand to establish the racial status of the accused. She testified that Sockum and Harmon were cousins, and Sockum was again found guilty as charged.

His birthright having been stripped away, Levin Sockum became a bitter man and soon sold his store and moved to Gloucester, New Jersey. At some point the family added a terminal "e" to their name and thereafter pronounced it "Sock-yoom."

Levin lies at rest in a family plot in Cedar Grove Cemetery in Gloucester. Now largely illegible, his weathered tombstone bears the inscription:

> Levin Sockume
> Died Dec 25, 1864
> Aged 57 yrs
> I have fought a good fight
> I have finished my work
> And I have kept the faith

A monument to Lydia Clark was erected in 1927 by the National Society of Colonial Dames in Delaware. It stands on Delaware Road 312 at Clark Avenue in Oak Orchard and gives the year of Lydia's death as 1859, but Lydia actually died in 1856, less than a year after the trial.

Clark's lonely grave, set deep in a pine woods, was marked by a crude stone, apparently provided by the Burtons. The inscription it bears reflects the intolerance of its day:

> In memory of
> Lydia Clark
> Who died Dec. 26, 1856
> Aged about 75 years
> The last one of the Aborigines
> of the Country, a person of
> truth and a witness against
> the arrogant negroes that
> assumed to be what they
> were not

I have not been able to conclusively resolve the conflicting statements about Lydia's age. If she was five or six at the outset of the American Revolution, as Fisher indicated, then she would have been eighty-five or eighty-six at the time of her death.

Chief William Russell Clark, Lydia's great grandson, was born the same year the trial was held. His father, James H. Clark, told him that Lydia was dependent on the Burtons for food and shelter and was coerced to appear in court. Because of her fierce pride in her Indian ancestry, it must have been difficult for her to swear under oath that she was a blood relative of Harmon and Sockum and then testify as to their African-American bloodline.

Concerned that Lydia's grave site might be destroyed, Chief Charles C. Clark, son of William Russell, obtained permission in the latter half of the twentieth century to exhume it.

Charles' son, Chief Kenneth Clark, told me several years ago: "My dad had her remains moved to his backyard. We have the tombstone in the garage. It was broke. We were going to get it sandblasted and put it back up, but we've never done that."

When I asked Chief Clark about his great, great, great grandmother and told him I was interested in writing about her, he replied, "Everything has been written about her that possibly could have been written. I don't think there's anything that you can enlarge upon. It comes to a point where different people said this and that, and there's nothing to back up what was said. Who knows. It's inflammatory towards a lot of people and some things are better left alone. It's just the way things were at that time."

Since I first spoke to Kenneth Clark, he and his son, Charles C. Clark IV, have resigned their posts as chief and assistant chief of the Nanticoke Indian Association, ending their family's eighty-year involvement in the organization. Kenneth had held the post for nearly thirty-one years and Charles for more than a decade.

"A Clark has served as chief of the Nanticoke tribe for more than a hundred and twenty years," Kenneth Clark said after his resignation, "and we have led the Nanticoke Indian Association since its inception in 1922." And then he added: "The non-Indian actions, disrespect of our ancestors' ways and so much more that we and our supporters have endured for several years have left us no choice other than to back away."

Because the Clarks strongly support the Nanticokes' longstanding claim to be the only remnants of Delaware's original inhabitants, recent efforts by the Lenape Tribe to gain state recognition have caused dissent, and the dispute has been aggravated by a controversial archaeological report that concluded the Sussex County Nanticokes are "genealogically indistinguishable" from members of the Cheswold Lenape.

Attempts had been made at the January 2002 election meeting of the Nanticoke Association to remove the Clarks from office, but after a fight over proxy votes that lasted until 1:30 a.m., they again emerged victorious.

"The elections prove that a group within the tribe will stop at no lengths to further their agenda," Charles Clark said. "That agenda places family interests and loyalties above what is best for the Nanticoke tribe."

According to Charles, the split is "between those who uphold the requirement that members must be able to trace their ancestry to the 1881 tribal rolls and those who are upset that their cousins and second cousins cannot join. If the integrity of the tribal rolls is not maintained, federal recognition will be impossible."

But there may be more than membership requirements involved in the dispute. Some association members have opposed Charles Clark's efforts to adopt customs from other tribes. In the summer of 2001, Charles hosted an eight-day Lakota ceremony known as the sun dance. Three Nanticokes and twenty Native Americans from other tribes participated. Clark said that he hoped the incorporation of such traditions would "reinvigorate and revive the spirit of our people."

The backlash took the Clarks by surprise. "It was amazing," Charles said. "We were called devil worshippers by some of our people."

Charles Clark has issued an open invitation for others to join him. "Those who want to stick with what's important, people who want to truly uphold the Nanticoke name, we're banding together;

we're sticking together," he said. "A membership card in the Nanticoke Indian Association is not what's important. What's important is that Indian identity be written on the heart."

Whether the great grandsons of Nau-Gwa-Ok-Wa will eventually emerge as leaders of a separate group is not clear at the moment. Their opponents call them "chiefs without a tribe."

Chief William Russell Clark, Center, and Charles C. Clark, Right, at Lydia Clark's Monument in 1927

Above: John Lewis' Store

Below: John Lewis Making Change

Tales from the College of Knowledge

When my book *Conversations in a Country Store* was published, many readers incorrectly assumed that I had collected the material at John Lewis' Store. The Cornersville landmark, west of Cambridge on Route 343, has achieved a legendary status on Maryland's Eastern Shore, both for the service it provides and for the folks who gather there.

"I went in and out for the first sixteen years of my life," writer Helen Chappell told me. "My father [a Philadelphia surgeon who owned property and hunted in Dorchester County] used to sit down with the watermen and farmers. The tale telling would begin, and I would listen. I really think that was where I got my start as a writer. As far as I'm concerned, Lewis' Store is a national treasure. Old Mr. Lewis scooped the best ice cream cones anywhere. But the magic for me as a kid was the parking lot. It was paved in bottle caps. My brother and I thought that was just neat."

Because so many stories about the hundred-and-twenty-six-year-old establishment have been circulated throughout Maryland and beyond, it is sometimes difficult to separate fact from fancy. The demeanor of the individual who shared the following anecdote suggested that I could depend upon every word to be the unimpeachable truth.

"A woman stopped at the store one morning on her way somewhere and told John to have her husband pick up a quart of milk when he came by. When the man didn't show up at his usual time—he was one of the regulars—John figured he must have had an accident, so he called 911 and had an ambulance sent to the house. Of course the man was fine. He had just been catching up on a few chores. Somebody asked John if that was really true, and he said, 'Nah, that ain't the way it was. She wanted him to bring a loaf of bread.'"

After the storekeeper had concluded an evening of reminiscing before a packed house in the Visitors' Center at Backwater National Wildlife Refuge, I confronted him with the ambulance tale.

"No," Lewis emphatically denied the alleged incident with an incredulous expression on his face, "that never happened."

He should not have been surprised by such a fabrication. Much wilder ones are spun on the benches in his store every day.

"As far as I can find out," Lewis had begun his informal address, "the store got built in 1876 by a fellow named George Kirby. Sam LeCompte ran it in the early 1900s, followed by Sam Spedden, Frank Norris, Henry and Carol Thomas, Earl Webb and Buck Evans. Then we took over the first day of February in 1947—my father and mother and myself.

"Everything went well for the first year, and then Mr. John Truitt came into the picture. He said to my father: 'John, there's a store in Cambridge. Why don't you open that up?'

"So we had two going at the same time. My mother ran the one in Cambridge and my father ran the one down where we are today. Cambridge was a drive-in, and we had anywhere from eighteen to twenty-five boys and girls working. We worked three shifts a day, starting at six o'clock in the morning till eleven at night, and that was seven days a week. I helped my mother there, and I helped my father back and forth. I was a 'go-for' in between.

"Then, in 1959 my father passed away and my mother said, 'Which store do you want to keep?'

"I said, 'Mother, let's you and I take the one down to the country.' I said, 'I'll go down and open it up in the morning, and you come in at eleven-thirty or twelve o'clock. You stay till six and I'll come back then and stay till eleven at night.'

"I didn't realize it at the time, but I went in retirement. Every afternoon I hunted and fished, and it was a really nice hobby. I enjoyed myself and had a lot of friends, especially when I furnished the boat, the bait, the tackle—everything.

"Then, in 1976 my mother had her leg amputated, and that's when I had to take over by myself. But it was always a family store."

Lewis has two brothers and two sisters, and while they have each pursued their own careers and lived in other communities, the family has remained close. His brothers, Jimmy and Bill, now provide welcome relief during the long workweek.

In 1953 John married Shirley Hurley, and together they raised three daughters. One lives in California, one in Cambridge and one next door to her parents. "She's more or less a standby," Lewis said, referring to the latter.

"I've got a wonderful family—brothers, sisters, children, nieces, nephews—and they all fall in and help me whenever I need help. I really love them.

"I do many things and I try to help people," Lewis modestly told his Blackwater audience. "Every week there's two or three ladies whose cars won't start—a couple of things. I call my buddies and they come to the rescue.

"About a month ago, a lady called me. She said, 'Mr. Lewis, I got a blacksnake. Come on down here.'

"I said, 'Just a few minutes.'

"I took a shotgun and went up, killed the snake and made her happy.

"That's the story of the store. We try to help everybody there is. It's a place where anybody can call day or night and get help, and I like it that way. It's just a cheerful thing.

"In 1947 I bought the third television that was sold in Cambridge by Applegarth Brothers, which was an RCA. It had an eight-inch screen. Then I got a twelve-inch magnifying glass and put it on the shelf. Every night the store was loaded with the older people. Back in them days the older people spent more time in stores than the younger people. We had wrassling on there and baseball games. Sometimes you couldn't tell if it was a ball or a strike, but they all had a good time.

"There was an old timer named Mr. George Robbins. He was like a lot of us—didn't have much money—so he used to wear overalls, and he'd wrap newspaper around his legs for insulation. He sounded like the tin man walking along. He'd come in the store and set back there.

"So one day a state trooper came in, and he asked Mr. Robbins: 'Does anybody speed down here?'

"'Heh?' George said.

"The trooper says, 'Do they speed down here?'

"George had an old jug, and he'd went a couple doors down the road to fill it with water. He said, 'They go so damn fast on this road, they suck the water right out my jug.'

"So the trooper come down and arrested about eight or ten people and got them to slow down.

"A lot happens in the store. Some things I can't even say."

For years, Neck District residents have referred to their rural market and gathering place as the "College of Knowledge" and more recently as "Lewis University." I've seen business cards bearing the latter title.

John Lewis had not traveled alone to Blackwater. Several of his "students"—long-standing regulars at the institution—had made the journey with their "professor" and were seated on a store bench they had brought for the occasion. Nearly half-an-hour into the program, a gentleman quietly slipped into the auditorium and joined them.

"I see a fellow just come in here," John wryly observed. "He's the new man—Phil Wagner. The only way he can find his way around Dorchester County is to tie little yellow ribbons on bushes. I was looking for them yellow ribbons coming down tonight. He's been putting them out since last Thursday, and he hadn't got this far. That's why he's late.

"We've had quite some experiences," Lewis remarked, returning to his retrospect. "We had a fellow used to come in the store named

Earl Prichett, and he had an experiment. He said you can take a glass milk bottle and stuff it full of absorbent cotton. Then you take a .45 pistol and shoot down into it, and you can pick the bullet up.

"Well, I got on the telephone and called Benny Phillips. I said, 'Benny, you have any old glass milk bottles?'

"He said, 'Yeah, Johnny, I got one over here. Why?'

"I said, 'You don't want to know.'

"So I went over to his house and got the milk bottle. We stuffed it up with swathing cotton, and I went and got my pistol. I loaded her and I said, 'Earl, you got the honor of shooting in this jar. Then we'll take the bullet out.'

"He shot, and he drove that bottle down in the ground so far we never did find the bullet.

"And then we had Sherwood Wright, which passed away now. He said, 'You take a one-by-six plank—a seasoned board—and you take your hammer and drive a nail in with one whack. So what we did, we had an experiment with that."

Motioning to one of his students, Lewis said, "This is Arthur Wheatley. He keeps the history. I call on Arthur and he brings back all the memories and keeps us well informed.

"One day we had a big, heavy rain, and I asked the bunch in the store: 'How much rain did you get last night?'

"Some said one inch; another said two.

"Clarence Keys came in the store and he said, 'Well, I went out and looked, and I had three inches on the clothes line.'

"The fertilizer companies in Cambridge will call me and say, 'How much rain did you have?' I'll always have somebody in the store or around and about, and they can tell us pretty well.

"Like this morning I had one and a half tenths. Phil had six and a half tenths, Dave Wheatley had six tenths and Robert Bramble had six tenths. We get together all the information and put it down on paper.

"So Jack at the fertilizer company called me up and said, 'Johnny, how much rain did you get down there?' I give him what we got and down he come and sprayed the fields—some of them. One he got stuck in.

"We had a fellow used to come down named Jim Reeves. He was over on Capitol Hill, and he'd bring a lot of senators and congressmen. He had a duck blind he rented from Billy's father. This one morning he come down, and he had a congressman fellow from New Jersey. It was five o'clock in the morning. I was writing up his gunning license and he kept hollering, 'Mister, I hope you got change; I hope you got change!'

"Well, I thought he had something.

"So when it come his turn to pay, he had a hundred-dollar bill.

"I said, 'My Lord, mister, children down here use this for play money.'

"I've had governors down and I've had presidents down. President Carter comes just about every year, 'round about Thanksgiving. Jody Powell used to be his press secretary, and he has a farm down at Martin Neck."

Behind one of the store benches hangs a "Jimmy Carter for President" poster that bears the hand-penned inscription: "To my friend John Lewis." It is signed: "Jimmy Carter."

"Generally, the Secret Service will come in three or four days in advance and look all around the store. They've been there enough now, they hardly walk around anymore. They come in and say, 'How you doing?'

"The fellow who's head of security in Baltimore—we got pretty chummy. He said, 'You do more investigating of me than I do of you.'

"Anytime a stranger comes in the neighborhood, I always try to jot the tag number down in case something goes wrong and the police come. The sheriffs come in quite often. In one case, a fella had rented his house to a friend, and his friend's son came down and broke in and robbed him. Well, I had his tag number, and in a few days they had him.

"I had a group in there this morning from Idaho. I asked the lady if she had any potatoes. She said she brought plenty of them with her.

"And there was a man in the store today from Kuwait. He's with the U. S. Embassy in Kuwait.

"Week before last I had a lady from South Africa. She was from the National Democratic Headquarters. I've had folks from Argentina, Chile, Paraguay, Africa, Britain—worldwide. There's something different every day."

When John mentioned that he offers free coffee to patrons every morning, a woman in the audience interrupted: "About thirty-nine years ago I moved down to the Neck District. I'm married to Phillip, and he brings me out of Cambridge and takes me down to the end of Cook Point. Every Saturday he would leave me and go out to John Lewis' Store, and it was open till about eleven o'clock at night. It just about come to a divorce. What was taking him out to John Lewis' store was that every Saturday night they would have homemade cakes out there. Johnny would furnish the cake and soda so the men could sit around and talk. Weren't any women out there. I think there weren't, anyway."

"At the fire company," Lewis explained, "they had a cake they raffled off every Saturday night, and mostly they had men there. We had ninety-nine percent of the chances. So they'd ask who won the cake, and I'd treat them to soft drinks—anything they want to drink."

"We only lost one, John," a student injected, "and they brought it back. Dr. Fell's wife took it home and then brought it back."

"Do you do much heckling of each other?" a member of the audience wanted to know.

"Oh, my Lord!" Lewis replied. "If you can't wear the shoes, don't put them on."

"I've been going to Lewis University for forty-seven years," one of the students offered. "I enjoy it, but I haven't passed yet. I don't think I'll ever make it."

"I was told that the store was the College of Knowledge," a member of the Blackwater audience injected. "When did you get accredited as a university?"

"There is always somebody calling for information," John Lewis responded, "and if we don't have it, we can soon get it.

"Last year a fella went down to Atlanta, Georgia, to a conference down there, and he fell in love with stuffed jalapino olives. He looked all around and couldn't find them, so he came up and said, 'I've found something I really like—stuffed jalapino olives.'

"I said, 'I've never heard of them.'

"I looked in the grocery catalogs and seen olives, but no jalapinos. So I called my friend Bruce Bernard. 'Bruce,' I said, 'can you help me out? I got a man is looking for stuffed jalapino olives.'

"He said, 'I don't know; let me look.'

"So he got on the Internet, and the next day he called me and said, 'I found them up in New Jersey. How many do you want?'

"I said, 'He wants two cases.'

"He said, 'O.K., they're on the way.'

"About two, three days later, UPS came and, sure enough, I had two cases of jalapino olives.

"Anything you want, we can pretty well find it. I had one lady wanted Bon Ami Soap. It used to be a great thing. Before Windex and all that stuff, the women around here had Bon Ami Soap. You could just smear it on and wipe it off, and you got a nice, bright window. I got ahold of somebody out West had it. I sent them a check—which they waited a couple of weeks for it cleared—and they sent me my Bon Ami.

"One guy came in and said to me: 'What is it you don't have in this store?'

"I said, 'Well, I don't have no horseshoe nails.'

"So he happened to go up in Lancaster, Pennsylvania, and in about a week, here he comes with horseshoe nails. He brought me a whole box.

"We're always ready to help out where we can. Mr. Bob was out in Montana last year and Billy was supposed to pick him up at BWI [Baltimore Washington International Airport]. Well, something happened and his flight got in a little early. Mr. Bob has one of these new telephones. You don't have to plug it in the wall; you just pick it up. He was on the plane, and he called me and said, 'Johnny, I'm in trouble.'

"I said, 'What's the matter?'

"He said, 'Billy's supposed to meet me in Baltimore at six o'clock, and we're gonna arrive two hours early.'

"I said, 'O.K., I'll put the university to work.'

"So I got on the telephone and started calling around, and lucky enough, I found the restaurant where Billy was eating his lunch. I said, 'Billy, cut your lunch short; Mr. Bob's on his way—flying right now. Get up to Baltimore and pick him up.'

"That's one of the many services of the university. We always try and do something to help somebody."

"We have a rule at our house," a voice from the audience inject- ed. "If there's a problem, you call the store first, then you dial 911. John saved my husband's life when he had a heart attack. I wasn't home and he called the store, and John got an ambulance down there for him."

"The Maryland State Police call me quite often," Lewis returned to his reminiscence, "especially if someone passes away and they have a family member living down there. They'll ask me if I mind going down and delivering the message. I don't like to knock on somebody's door and tell them their uncle's in trouble or their aunt passed away. It's really a sad occasion to have to go, but I have did it quite a few times. I've been there fifty-six years now, and in fifty-six years you get a lot of chance.

"Like being a pallbearer—three times in one day is the most I ever was. I've got every afternoon off, so Mr. Thomas and Mr. Le-Compte [undertakers] will say, 'Call Johnny.'

"I don't like to say no to nobody if I can possibly do it. If I can help anybody at anytime, day or night, I'm only too willing to go and help them."

"To give an example of that," one of the Lewis brothers injected, "I pitch in and help John once in a while. One Saturday I was in the store and this gentleman come in. I said, 'May I help you?'

"He said, 'I hope you can.'

"I said, 'Well, what can I do for you?'

"He said, 'I'm looking for someone.'

"I said, 'Well, who are you looking for?'

"He said, 'I don't know.'

"I said, 'O.K., what's their address?'

"He said, 'I don't know that either.'

"The next question I asked, I said, 'Where are you from?'

"He said, 'Washington, D.C.'

"I said, 'You're down here looking for someone and you don't know who they are or where they are.'

"He said, 'That's right.'

"I said, 'What do you do?'

"He said, 'I'm a pilot for American Airlines, and I was flying over here last week and saw some restoration being done and some bulkheading. I know it's in this area.'

"I said, 'I'll call my brother John.'

"So I got John to the store, and in fifteen minutes we had him where he wanted to get to.

"Another time I was helping John in the store, and this fellow come in and said a man had passed away the night before.

"We have a lady who calls every day to talk and get the news. She mentioned this gentleman, so I said, 'He passed away last night.'

"Later on, I started getting phone calls: 'Is it true?'

"I said, 'Yep, that's what I heard.'

"Then, early in the afternoon, word got to me that the gentleman hadn't passed away; they had just declared him brain dead. So I called this lady. I really made her day because she loves the phone. So all the people she had called up that morning to tell them the man had died, she had to call back and say he hadn't.

"Then word came down about four-thirty that afternoon that now he had died, so I had to call her back again. Anyway, she was worn out by the end of the day."

"Tell them the story about the fish pond," a student prompted from the bench.

"Well," John Lewis responded, "Shirley [Mrs. Lewis]—she's got a fishpond. She enjoys Koi fish. So last year she said to me: 'I found a nice article on Japan. You want to go?'

"I said, 'I ain't lost nothing in Japan.'

"She said, 'I want to go.'

"I said, 'Well, go ahead.'

"So she sent off and got the tickets. She had all these check-list chores I had to do, and she said, 'I want you to take care of these fish.'

"I said, 'O.K.'

"On a Thursday before she left on Monday, she called me up crying. I thought somebody got murdered. We had fourteen of them Koi fish—bottoms up. I said, 'I don't know what happened to them, but I'm glad it happened before you left.'

"So she called down to the University of Maryland at Horns Point [Center of Environmental and Estuarine Studies] and got ahold of a gentleman down there. He said, 'Well, I'm pretty jammed up,' but he understood the predicament—she was crying and all— so he said, 'I'll be right down.'

"He come with his testers and stuff, and it was a lack of oxygen. And that's the story of the fish pond."

"No, it's not!" objected the student.

"Well," Lewis picked up the story, "I went out there the night before last. My daughter stopped over to Southern States and bought these little goldfish, and they had multiplied like monkeys. So I said, 'Well, I'll go feed the fish.' I walked around and stepped on one of those stones. It broke loose from the mortar and over in the pond I went. When I went to take a bath, I took my pants off and I had four goldfish in my pocket."

"That's the one I wanted to hear. Now tell them about that time you broke your arm giving directions,"

"I had a fellow come in from up in Pennsylvania. He was hauling lime and I was trying to tell him how to get out to Ross Neck. I jumped up on the bench, and when I jumped up, that bench kicked out from underneath of me and I broke my arm. I said, 'Damn if I ain't broke my arm.'

"He said, 'No!'

"I said, 'Yes, I have.'

"So I had to run in to the hospital, and Dr. McCarter put a cast onto it. He said, 'Take a rubber ball after about three or four days and exercise your hand. Well, he didn't know that was my hand that worked the cash resister and I didn't need no ball. He said, 'You've healed better than anybody I ever had.'"

And that isn't the only time that Lewis has suffered a broken arm, a prompting from the bench revealed.

"Now this is a true story," John began his tale of the second break. "At the time, I was opening at five o'clock. Like anybody else, I'm always rushing. I cleaned the windshield off—getting the frost off—and I started up to the store."

But the storekeeper was having difficulty seeing through the windshield. He had the driver's-side window rolled down, the door partly ajar, and he was peering out through the opening.

"Jackson happened to be coming up the road behind me, and when his lights hit that mirror, it scared me so bad I whipped the wheel, and it throwed me out of that car just like a slingshot. I had a brand new pair of corduroy pants on, and it tore the pants up and I broke my arm. The car went across the ditch, went across the field there and went across another ditch. Carl Morris happened to be looking, and he thought it was coming through his window, but it stopped before it got to his house.

"So a state trooper come to the store and I told him what happened. The bunch in there said, 'Are you gonna give him a ticket?'

"He said, 'I can't.'

"They said, 'What do you mean?'

"He said, 'He left the scene before the accident happened.'

"So that's how I got out of that one.

"Then I had a fellow up in Secretary painting the store one time, and he said to me: 'I want to get started early.'

"I said, 'All right, I'll pick you up at six o'clock.'

"So Bill was going to work at that time. I said, 'You start and I'll race you.' He had a little stake-back truck and I had a station wagon.

"So up the route we went. We got past Lovers Lane, which is just down past Dalesville a little bit, and I seen this car turn around. I said, 'Oh, oh.'

"It was Cecil Parks, the state trooper. I seen him when he made the circle but Bill didn't see him. I slacked off and let Cecil go by.

Bill kept on going. I said to myself, 'When I go by him, I'll blow the horn.'

"So when I got up there, Trooper Parks waved me in too. 'Oh, I got the Lewis brothers,' he said.

"I said, 'What's going on?'

"He says, 'I'll be back to take care of you in a few minutes.'

"So he went up and give Bill a warning, and he came back and give me a warning. So I got off that pretty good.

"One day Johnny Keys forgot something and he called and said, 'Now hurry up.'

"So I shot down there—man, I was going. And who did I meet? Cecil! He had radar. I shot right by him like I didn't even see him, and he come after me.

"'Buddy,' I said, 'what can I do for you?'

"He said, 'You know how fast you were going?'

"I said, 'I have no idea. Johnny told me to hurry up and I was rushing.'

"He said, 'You want to see? I got it right here on radar.'

"I said, 'Just erase it if you will.'

"So I got by that time.

"Johnny Keys was a good friend of mine. He passed away about twelve years ago. Every year they have a sale down at the fire company—the first weekend in November. Johnny got down there one year. He had a little bottle along and he lost his false teeth.

"Next morning he called the fellows he'd been down to the bar with and said, 'I've lost my false teeth,' but they hadn't seen them.

"So then he called down to the firehouse. He was too embarrassed to go down. Walt Taylor was the auctioneer, so Johnny told him: 'Look through the pockets of the suits and see if you can find any teeth into them.'

"Walt used to play jokes like the rest of us and he said, 'Ladies and gentlemen, before we start the sale today, we have a gentleman who lost his teeth down here last night.' He said, 'I'd like for everybody to look out for them, and especially look in the soup.'

"Anyhow, he'd lost them at home, and the next morning he got himself together and the dog come in with his teeth."

When this story was first published in *Tidewater Times*, I wrote: "There is no end to this story. If you would like to become part of it, go to the intersection of Race and Washington Streets in Cambridge and drive west on Washington (Maryland Route 343) for nine miles to Cornersville. You will find Lewis' Store on your right, just beyond the community."

Everything, of course, comes to an end—or at least changes—and on Thursday, July 15, 2004, *The* (Cambridge) *Daily Banner* carried the following "Guest Opinion."

As a country storekeeper for the last 57 years in the Neck District on MD 343, west of Cambridge, it is very difficult for me to express the gratitude and feelings of thanks that I have for you letting me be part of your lives those many years.

A country store is a very unique place in that you have the opportunity to get to know the community and its people in a very special way. I have known families from the great-grandparents, grandparents, parents, the children.

This is also true with many of our neighbors who have moved into the area and sat on the bench and related a little of their family history with me.

This has been a wonderful experience for me. For not only have I gotten to know you as customers, it has been my pleasure to know you as friends.

I know, as the years have come and gone, the appearance of the store has not always been what I would have liked it to be, but at the same time, I always thought that it was more important to make all feel that they were part of what the community was all about.

I really tried to answer all requests, not only for the products that I may not have had on the shelves, but also where they could find the various services needed from the private and government sector.

Many people have asked me about the store being known as "Lewis University." This came about from the Rev. Lewis (no relation) coming to the store and listening to many of the topics that were discussed. He said that this was a place you could really learn about yourself.

We are all lucky to be part of a community that has a great volunteer fire company and E.M.T. team. There are three very good churches: Beckwith, Speddens, and St. Johns. Through them, more pleasure than you can imagine. There was one person that I will mention that sums up what went on at the store, and that was John Keys.

I know that many of you did not know John, but for the ones that did, I will tell you that he was one of a kind, and if for no other reason, you should become part of going to the store in case another John Keys comes along.

Thank you and may God bless you.

—John Lewis

John Robertson and John Lewis on "The Bench"

Fujiyama

On a Christmas Long Ago

There is no feeling in this world that compares to standing on an icy perch high above the earth, buffeted by winds and so close to the sky that you want to reach out and touch it. I have never engaged in technical rock climbing, nor have I conquered any significant mountain in the world, but some of the best moments of my life—and the worst—have been spent at high elevations, and I *have* reached out and touched the sky.

It is difficult for most Americans to comprehend Japanese spiritualism. There is no proper equivalent for the term "Shinto" in English. Shinto or Kaminomichi is an almost indefinable religious persuasion. It is the way of the kami—the way of the gods—and has been observed by the Japanese from time immemorial.

Shinto is not a set of theories or judgments; it is an all-pervading way. Its tenets contain neither grand philosophy nor complicated ritual. It is a religion of the heart, a creative or formative principle of life that has shaped Japanese culture, ethics, art, family and even national structure. It is a personal religion that ascribes divine attributes to every being and object, a kind of pantheism and highly sophisticated form of animism.

Kami are seen as divine forces of nature that take the form of objects and sometimes even concepts. Wind, rain, mountains, trees, rivers are all inhabited and guided by kami. Humans become kami after death and are revered by their descendants. Amaterasu, the sun goddess and ancestor of the imperial family, stands supreme above all kami; but nothing in nature is without spirit and power, and the Japanese will tell you that even the wishes of the tiniest insect can be heard in heaven.

Fujiyama, literally Fuji Mountain, rises to an altitude of 12,388 feet above the Plains of Edo, southwest of Tokyo. (Fuji is a type of spun silk fabric.) With the basic understanding of Shintoism that I have outlined above, you can appreciate why this majestic volcano is sacred to the Japanese. To those who live in its shadow, Fuji is a magical, living thing, and largely due to paintings, woodblock prints and photographs that have depicted its magnificence for centuries, it is the very symbol of Japan to people the world over.

The Japan Travel Bureau recently informed me that more than 200,000 people (30% of them foreigners) now climb Fujiyama each year between mid July and the end of August, when weather is stable and the mountain free of snow and ice. To view sunrise from Fuji's summit is considered one of Japan's most inspiring experiences.

If you inquire at tourist offices during the other ten months of the year, officials will say you cannot climb, but if you are properly equipped and submit a reasonable agenda, a permit can be acquired.

Mr. Kuroda was a Japanese engineer employed by the United States Air Force during the Korean War. In the early stages of World War II, he had assisted his own government in designing the fortifications on Iwo Jima, where 6,821 American and more than 20,000 Japanese soldiers, sailors and airmen died during thirty-six days of intense fighting in February and March, 1945. The flag raising on Surabachi—Iwo's volcano—is our best-known photograph of the war.

"There is an old saying," Kuroda-san told me shortly after we met: "'He who comes to Japan and does not climb Mount Fuji is a fool.' You must climb Fuji before you leave."

After I had stood on its summit for a second time during my first year and a half in the Far East, my Japanese friend pulled me aside and said, "I told you once that anyone who comes to Japan and does not climb Fuji is a fool, but we also have a second saying: 'He who climbs Fuji more than once is a greater fool.'"

In those days I planned my mountain adventures poorly, usually climbed alone and pushed ahead with the blind assumption that things would somehow come out O.K. Only an idiot ignores the fact that climbing is a serious game; ignore it long enough and you will surely pay a price.

A truce was signed with North Korea and China in 1953, ending three years of war, and I was scheduled to return to the States early in 1954. I longed for one more climb and decided to summit Fuji again, this time with her slopes garmented in ice and snow. Christmas seemed the perfect occasion.

Dick Mather is a descendant of Cotton Mather (1663-1728), an outspoken Puritan cleric and prolific author who is best remembered for the sanction he gave to the Salem witch trials. Dick was a rugged, independent soul who, like me, spent every free minute investigating those mystical islands where the war had sent us. "Gone native" is how our fellow airmen often described us.

Although we were friends, Dick and I had nearly always traveled alone, but I decided it would be prudent to have company on a winter assault of Fuji and invited him to join me. His immediate grin was enough to seal our pact. We gathered clothing and gear: long johns, wool shirts, trousers, jackets, insulated boots, down-filled parkas and sleeping bags, caps, gloves and mitts, backpacks, goggles, crampons, ice axes, rope, rations, canteens and water, two small cans of Sterno fuel for heating food and melting snow, matches and a camera.

With sunlight still faintly caressing the western flank of her peak on the afternoon of December 23, Fuji's massive, hoary cone rose like a fairytale image across a panorama of rice paddies, blurred by the speed of our electric train and rapidly fading in the gathering dusk.

"Isn't it beautiful?" a middle-aged woman sitting next to me in a bright kimono whispered in Japanese as we admired the view.

"Yes," I nodded. "Fuji is a wonderful mountain," but I knew that we looked upon the scene with very different emotions. For the first time, I could see and feel the danger as well as the beauty.

When we disembarked at the Fujiyoshida station, darkness had fallen, and lodging and dinner were arranged at the first hostelry we encountered. I was anxious to disappear under the quilts in our un-heated room and attempt some sleep, but my partner refused to re-tire until he had located the kami that he believed to inhabit the chamber, and he consumed a very long time with his search.

Dick's involvement in some elements of Japanese culture far exceeded mine. Just before our climb, he had attended a shrine ceremony and participated in walking across beds of hot coals. The fact that he had not yet washed the charcoal from his feet had something to do with attaining good fortune on our impending climb. I have forgotten the details.

The morning of December 24 dawned calm and cloudless. We gulped a cold breakfast of C-rations, shouldered our packs and strode out of town on an unpaved road into one of the most beauti-ful panoramas the world has to offer. Like two stallions escaped from their coral, we put the few miles of flat countryside quickly behind us and entered a trail that rose, gently at first, through the timber blanketing Fuji's lower slopes.

While gathering my thoughts to write this, I could not recall the distance from Fujiyoshida to the mountain, so I dashed off an e-mail question to the Japan Travel Bureau.

"The direct distance between Fujiyoshida City and the peak of Mt Fuji," came a quick reply, "is 15 kilometers [9.32 miles] on the map, but if you follow the tortuous trail to reach the summit, the distance is much longer."

Well up into the timber, we encountered a small hut that almost straddled the trail, and an elderly man greeted us with hands raised to block our passage. "No, no, no," he repeated, "You cannot go on Fuji. Too dangerous. It is ice."

"It's all right," I told him; "we're well prepared." And we simply stepped around the protesting little man, who would easily have fit under my armpit.

With spirits high, we reached the ice field sometime after noon, pausing there to rope up and strap crampons to our boots. Neither of us had ever climbed on sheer ice before, and the sheet rising before us into the sky was hard and glistening. The spikes had to be planted with force, and their grip seemed tenuous at best.

Neither had we been trained in the use of a rope, and the chord that joined us constantly got in our way. After raising further concern that we would not be able to belay each other on such treacherous footing in the event of a fall, the tackle came off and was returned to my pack. It would be each man for himself.

I was to his right and slightly below when Dick slipped. It all happened with the quickness of lightning, but I can still "hear" the thud as he fell and the whooshing scrape of his parka against the ice as he slid past me, just an arm's length out of reach. By a combination of instinct and good fortune, he was able to arrest the uncontrolled glissade, and we continued upward, more alert from a rush of adrenalin.

Nowhere else can weather change as quickly as on a mountain. Within a span of fifteen minutes, our environment shifted from blue sky and sunshine to a thick overcast that soon flung sleet in our faces. Before we could discuss our plight, a blinding snowstorm had enveloped us.

Just ahead, partially dug into Fuji's flank, I could see a small hut, the only shelter of any description that we encountered during the climb—a tiny wart on the hip of a giant. Its low walls of unmortared stone were topped by crude timbers and overlaid with additional stone and cinder to keep them from blowing away. Rough boards nailed to a wooden frame sealed its narrow entrance.

It was clear that we needed shelter, and quickly. I began to pry at one of the boards with the chopping blade of my ice axe, then with the pick, then with the opposite end of the shaft—the one terminating in a metal point. In my haste to pry an opening, I carelessly applied too much pressure, and the wooden shaft snapped several inches above the spike. My heart sank. I had lost an important tool to maintain stability on the ice field, and the steepest part of the climb was yet to come.

With increased caution, we were able to remove several boards and crawled inside. The interior resembled a small cave—dark and cold and damp. After our eyes became accustomed to the gloom, we searched the chamber and discovered two drums containing several heavily quilted sleeping pads. We could not know then that gaining access to the hut and those mats would save our lives, but we well knew that fortune had smiled upon us.

Fully dressed, except for my boots, I crawled into my sleeping bag and pulled two of the quilts over me. There, curled in a fetal position, I spent the most frightening eighteen hours of my life, listening to the uninterrupted violence of what sounded like hurricane-force winds only a few feet away.

With the first gray light of Christmas dawn, I looked toward the opening we had forced. Beneath it, a sparkling drift rose in the stylized form of a Madonna holding a child in her arms. I am not one to make miracles of nature's coincidences, but the form served as a fitting and somehow comforting decoration until the continuously sifting snow converted it into just another mound of white.

Around mid-morning we crawled outside, intent on completing the climb, but with each faltering step or two, the wind tried to fling us into space. Often in absolute terror, I pressed my body against the mountain, clutching the shaft of my imbedded axe with both hands to keep from being blown away. After nearly two hours of the buffeting, we surrendered, exhausted, having advanced only a hundred feet from the hut.

An hour or so after dawn on December 26, the wind abated slightly, and we agreed to make one final try for the summit. Footing was treacherous and the advance slow. My face and hands and feet burned and ached, then grew numb from the cold. The swirling snow never let up. I have no recollection of how long we climbed.

Considering the whole of my life, reaching the summit of Fuji in that blizzard is the most physically challenging thing I have ever done, yet I felt no sense of triumph. We stood at the top of a nation, but our whole world was condensed to a tight, stinging fog of whirling snow and ice. With no higher step to take, exhaustion drove me to my knees, and at that moment I was certain I was going to die.

No terror accompanied the conclusion. I have never been so indifferent about death in my life. The thought of it was more appealing than frightening.

It is hard to recall the emotions, now dulled by the passage of half a century. Had I been alone, I feel certain I would have remained there. I suppose it was youthful pride as much as anything that forced me to get up. Even in my weakest moment, I couldn't stand to have Dick believe that I was a quitter.

You might believe that descending a mountain is easier than climbing it, but that is often not the case. While ascending a steep slope, you can lean into it. There is a sense of stability and usually something to grab if you need support. I have always felt much less secure when retreating and having to overcome my body's inclination to pitch downhill. On a steep slope, especially one covered with ice, you cannot simply walk down. Each step must be measured and deliberate, and a whole new set of muscles comes into play.

It surprised me how quickly we managed to relocate our shelter—that we found it at all in that world of white against white. We paused only long enough to retrieve our belongings. As I shouldered my pack, I took stock of my condition. I was able to move my fingers and exercise them inside my gloves and mitts, but my feet felt like two leaden appendages and I knew they were frostbitten. I also understood there was nothing I could do for them but get off the mountain as quickly as possible. That seemed doable now, and a modicum of strength and determination returned.

As we continued to descend, one small, calculated step after another, the intensity of the wind gradually diminished. Although the fiercest blizzard I have ever experienced had been raging for more than forty hours, nowhere could I have gathered enough snow on that icy slope to make a snowball. It had all settled below, sifting through the forest and blanketing the plains that stretched toward Tokyo.

By the time we entered timberline, the storm had finally moved on, and stars twinkled through the canopy of evergreens. It was dark when our boots crunched past the old man's hut, and a new day—December 27—had dawned when our train pulled into Tachikawa station.

Thanks to tender medical treatment, I lost none of my frost-bitten toes, but a lot of dead skin sloughed away and the darkened nails fell off after a few weeks.

Japanese friends informed me that weather instruments installed on the south rim of Fuji's summit had recorded temperatures of minus thirty-five degrees and winds as high as seventy miles per hour during the Christmas storm, and they presented me with a small article clipped from a Tokyo newspaper that bore the headline: "Two Americans Missing on Fuji."

Hadn't the old man seen our tracks in the snow? I asked my friends to inform whatever authorities might be interested that we had survived.

When I returned to the engineering office with frostbitten hands and face and wearing a pair of fleece slippers to ease the pain in my swollen feet, Kuroda-san just looked at me and shook his head. He had run out of sayings.

Postscript: I recently saw a photograph in which Fujiyama was scarred on one side by what appeared to be zigzagging strips of concrete, making their way upward from the tree line. I was horrified and wrote again to the Japan Travel Bureau: "Is there now a paved road to the summit of Fuji?"

"More you climb," came the astonishing reply, "more the slope becomes steep, so the road and the bus stops at 2500m [8,202 feet] high. You should then climb on foot up to the summit of Mt Fuji."

Commercialism, I suppose, will eventually conquer all the beauty on Earth.

The Author at the Edge of the Ice Field on Fujiyama

The Witch of Pungo

an's belief in witchcraft ranges back to ancient times, and
throughout most of the four thousand years that have
passed since the Code of Hammurabi was written, penal-
ties for practicing it have been harsh. "If a man has put a spell upon
a man and has not justified himself," the Babylonian law states, "he
that wove the spell shall be put to death."

Cotton Mather (1663-1728), Boston clergyman and prolific author, had much to say about witches. In his *Late Memorable Provi-
dences Relating to Witchcraft and Possessions*—penned when he was
twenty-two—Mather offered strong sanction to the Salem witch
trials and executions that would soon unfold.

"Go tell Mankind that there are Devils and Witches," he wrote.
"Go tell the world...what it is that these Monsters love to do. It has
been made a doubt by some whether there are any such things as
Witches...but the Word of God assures us that there have been
such, and gives order about them...."

Exodus 22:18: "Thou shalt not suffer a witch to live."

Quite simply, witches have historically been viewed as criminals
who work in supernatural ways to inflict harm on individuals and
their property.

The colonists' notion of witchcraft was, first of all, a religious

106

conviction. Belief in the devil and his omnipotence was paramount to one's belief in the power of a witch. To become a witch, one had to enter into a covenant with Satan; then, as his minion, a witch gained the ability to cause harm to others by supernatural means. A witch's malice might be directed towards people, animals, crops and domestic products. Among the latter, beer, cheese and butter are the most commonly cited. Traditionally, most witches have been women, but men have also been accused and tried.

Although most of the persecution of witches in America stains the archives of Puritan New England, religious convictions throughout the colonies embraced a belief in witchcraft, and that confidence became an integral part of the social order. The belief in witches and their power to harm was perpetuated for more than two centuries through a system of myths and rituals and has not entirely been lost today.

Residents and governments along the shores of Chesapeake Bay took a far more reasoned approach to the prosecution of accused witches than did the radical religious communities in New England. While several women were executed for the alleged practice of witchcraft aboard ships bound for Maryland and Virginia, Rebecca Fowler was the only tidewater resident ever to be sentenced to death and hanged. Her execution took place at St. Mary's City in Maryland in 1685.

One of the more fascinating witchcraft cases in the Chesapeake Bay region played out its drama along a coastline broken by numerous coves and inlets in Pungo Township, Princess Anne County, Virginia, in an area that is now part of Virginia Beach.

Grace White was born about 1660, the daughter of John and Susan White. It is recorded that John received a land patent of one hundred and ninety-five acres along Ashville Creek at the eastern end of Muddy Creek. Depending upon the season, he supported his family either by farming or carpentry.

Grace married James Sherwood around 1680, when records show that John White deeded fifty acres of land to his "loving son-in-law." John died the following year and bequeathed the remainder of his property to his daughter and her husband. It appears that

Grace was an only child.

We do not think of colonial women as possessing great beauty, but Grace White Sherwood is said to have been stunningly attractive. Apparently, she was also a strong-willed woman who commonly wore men's clothing and was unafraid to speak her mind. Because she possessed considerable knowledge about the use of herbs, she was known in Pungo Township as a healer.

The citizens of Pungo established a complex legend around Grace Sherwood during her lifetime, and those traditions have been substantially expanded in the years since her death. At this point in time, we cannot be certain which of the popular beliefs about her originated while she was alive and which came later as embellishments.

The fact that rosemary flourishes in Princess Anne County is attributed to Grace, and there are two versions of how she allegedly brought the herb to Virginia. Both begin with a desire to have some of its leaves to sweeten her lard.

In a single day, the first tale informs us, Grace sailed to England in an eggshell, procured a sprig of Rosemary and returned to Virginia that evening. No mention is made of the species of fowl whose egg she utilized in such a remarkable voyage.

The second version claims that she rowed in her eggshell to a ship lying at anchor in Lynnhaven Bay. Its crew, with the exception of a cabin boy, had gone ashore. Grace boarded the craft and enlisted the boy to weigh anchor and hoist the sails. She then cast a spell that caused a great wind to blow them to England in a matter of a few hours. There, she disembarked and gathered rosemary shrubs. Back on board, Grace reversed the wind and returned to the Chesapeake as quickly as she had departed. The cabin boy was left to anchor the ship and furl the sails while Grace rowed away in her eggshell. When the crew returned, it is claimed, they found the poor lad in a state of total exhaustion.

Whether rosemary was unknown in Princess Anne before Grace's time, I have no knowledge. It is native to regions around the Mediterranean.

In still another legend, Grace's neighbors are said to have once denied her request to accompany them on a picnic. As the haughty folks rowed across Currituck Sound in a dory, an eggshell passed them. When they eventually reached the far shore, they found the eggshell tied to a snag by a thread and Grace sitting in the shade of a tree, eating her lunch and cackling.

Witches and eggshells share a history. In P. P. Nyegosh's seventeenth century "The Mountain Wreath," the witch says:

> We meet on th' copper threshing-floor:
> And we alone know where it is;
> In March we ride on weaving-beams,
> Together hold our secret councils,
> Decide on whom to work our ill.
> Many a different form we take,
> And we row with silver oars;
> Of fragile eggshell is our boat....

I know someone who claims that he grew up under the admonition to always make a hole in the bottom of the shell after eating a boiled egg. That act, you see, will prevent a witch from using the shell to sail across the sea.

The first evidence that worries of witchcraft were afoot in Princess Anne County appears in its court records of 1655, when a "private court" assembled on May 23 in the home of Edward Hall of Lynnhaven and published the following statement. This document stands as further evidence that Virginia folks were cut from a more liberal cloth than those in Massachusetts. To make them easier for you to read and understand, I have edited each of the colonial documents quoted in this article.

"Whereas a number of dangerous and scandalous speeches have been raised by some persons concerning several women in this county and terming them to be witches, whereby their reputations have been impaired and their lives brought in question, it is by this court ordered that any person raising any such scandal concerning any party whatsoever, who shall not be able to prove the same, both upon oath and by sufficient witness, shall hereafter pay a thousand pounds of tobacco in the first place and likewise be liable to further censure of the court."

No one knows for certain how long Grace Sherwood was suspected of having practiced witchcraft or when accusations against her began. Her name appeared on Princess Anne County court records for the first time on March 3, 1697, when she and her husband brought a defamation suit against Richard Capps. The defendant had publicly claimed that Grace was a witch and accused her of casting a spell on his bull, causing it to die. The suit was dismissed when the parties settled privately.

Grace next appeared in court on September 10, 1698, when she and her husband filed additional defamation suits against two sets of defendants.

In the first case, the Sherwoods charged John and Jane Gisbourne with slander, declaring that they had wronged, defamed and abused Grace in her good name and reputation by accusing her of bewitching their cotton and causing a bad crop. After a short trial, jury foreman Christopher Cocke brought forth a verdict on behalf of the defendants.

The second action petitioned by the Sherwoods on September 10 was raised against Anthony and Elizabeth Barnes. Remember the name Elizabeth Barnes; we shall encounter it again.

Elizabeth had informed anyone willing to listen that she was awakened one night to find two figures dressed in black, standing near her bed. One was a tall male with the head of a goat and with glowing red eyes, obviously a reference to the devil. The other person was Grace Sherwood.

The male figure disappeared while Grace grew fangs and claws, forced Elizabeth out of bed, climbed on her back and rode her about the room until she collapsed from exhaustion. Then, according to Elizabeth's testimony, Grace "went out the keyhole or crack in the door like a black cat."

The Sherwoods presented seven witnesses over a period of four days, but after a jury had weighed all the testimony, foreman Francis Sayer announced another verdict in favor of the defendants. The Sherwoods were ordered to pay court costs as well as fees for the witnesses' time, room and board during the trial.

Grace next appeared on county records in 1701 when James Sherwood's last will and testament was probated. He left the farm to his wife, along with a small estate and three young sons to care for. The forty-year-old widow and mother could hardly have imagined that four years later she would be faced with even greater difficulties.

On December 7, 1705, Grace sued neighbor Luke Hill and his wife Uxor for "trespass of assault and battery." Grace claimed that Uxor had assaulted, bruised, maimed and barbarously beaten her, and she requested damages in the amount of fifty pounds sterling. The reason for the assault is not stated, but a jury awarded twenty shillings to Grace and ordered the Hills to pay court costs.

In response, Luke and Uxor filed formal accusations of witchcraft against Grace, which she apparently ignored because the following entry was made in court records on January 3, 1706: "Whereas Luke and Uxor Hill summoned Grace Sherwood to this court on suspicion of witchcraft, and she failing to appear, it is therefore ordered that the sheriff take her into custody to answer that summons in the next court."

On February 6, Luke Hill was directed to pay all fees relating to his complaint, and it was ordered that Grace be searched for the witch's mark by twelve women. The examination was conducted on March 7 by a jury whose foreman was none other than Elizabeth Barnes. Remember Elizabeth's bedtime tale?

The record reads: "Whereas a complaint has been made to the court by Luke Hill and his wife that one Grace Sherwood of this county has been suspected of witchcraft for a long time, the court summoned a jury of women to search her on the said suspicion, she assenting to the same. After the jury was impaneled and sworn and sent out to make due inquiry and inspection into all circumstances, and after they made a mature consideration, they brought in this verdict: 'We of the jury have searched Grace Sherwood and have found two things like tits with several other spots.'"

Perhaps doubting its authority to enter further judgment against Grace, the Princess Anne Court failed to respond to the jury's verdict, and Luke Hill took his complaint to Williamsburg.

At a hearing in Her Majesty's Royal Council on March 28, 1706, Hill reviewed his complaint that Grace Sherwood had bewitched his wife and requested that the attorney general of the colony be directed to prosecute her.

On April 16, the council responded with Attorney General Stephens Thompson's opinion, which read in part: "Upon perusal of the above order of this honorable Board, I do conceive and am of the opinion that the charge or accusation is too general and that the county court ought to make a further examination of the matters of fact."

On May 2, 1706, the Princess Anne Court issued an order to the county sheriff to take Grace into custody and further directed the Pungo constable to accompany the sheriff and "search the said Grace's house and all suspicious places carefully for all images and such like things as may in any way strengthen the suspicion."

Records dated June 7, 1706 reflect the court's displeasure over the fact that citizens selected to carry out a second search of Grace's body failed to appear for jury duty. They apparently feared that Grace would inflict harm on them.

"Whereas at the last court an order was passed that the sheriff should summon an able jury of women to search Grace Sherwood on suspicion of witchcraft, which, although the same was performed by the sheriff, yet they refused and did not appear. It is therefor ordered that the same persons be again summoned by the sheriff for their contempt, to be dealt with according to the utmost severity of the law, and that a new jury of women be by him summoned to appear next court to search her on the aforesaid suspicion, and that he likewise summon all evidence that he shall be informed of as material in the complaint, and that [Grace Sherwood] continue in the sheriff's custody unless she give good bond and security for her appearance at the next court, and that she be of good behavior towards her Majesty and all her liege people in the meantime."

Apparently, both the population of Princess Anne County and its court continued to have reservations about dealing with the accusations against Grace, as the following notation appears on court records dated July 5, 1706: "Whereas for several courts the business between Luke Hill and Grace Sherwood on suspicion of witchcraft have been for several things omitted, particularly for want of a jury to search her, and the court being doubtful that they should get one this court, and being willing to have all means possible tried either to acquit her or to give more strength to the suspicion that she might be dealt with as deserved, therefore it was ordered that this day, by her own consent, she be tried in the water by ducking, but the weather being very rainy and bad, so that possibly it might endanger her health, it is therefore ordered that the sheriff request the justices precisely to appear on Wednesday next by ten of the clock at the courthouse, and that he secure the body of the said Grace till that time."

In those dark ages of our history, it was common practice to "duck" persons suspected of witchcraft to determine their guilt or innocence. To prepare an individual for water trial, the right thumb of the accused was tied to the left big toe; then the left thumb was secured to the right big toe, and the individual was placed in deep water. If the defendant sank, she was believed to be innocent. Floating was a sign of rejection by the baptismal waters and certain proof that a covenant had been established between the accused and Satan.

The following excerpt is taken from the Princess Anne County Court Records of July 10, 1706. "Whereas Grace Sherwood, being suspected of witchcraft, has waited a long time for a fit opportunity for further examination, by her consent and the approbation of this Court, it is ordered that the Sheriff take all such convenient assistance of boat and men as he shall think fit, to meet at John Harper's Plantation in order to take the said Grace forthwith and put her into the water above man's depth and try her how she swims, therein always having care of her life to preserve her from drowning. And as soon as she comes out, he shall request as many ancient and knowing women as possibly he can to search her carefully for all teats, spots and marks about her body, not usual on others, and if they find the same, to make report to the court under oath to the truth thereof. And further, it is ordered that some women be requested to shift and search her before she goes into the water to determine that she carries nothing about her to cause any further suspicion."

While Grace has been described in folklore as a strong-willed woman who was unafraid to speak her mind, court records paint a somewhat contradictory picture: "Whereas on complaint of Luke Hill in behalf of her Majesty that now is against Grace Sherwood for a person suspected of witchcraft, and having had sundry evidences sworn against her, proving many circumstances to which she could not make any excuse or [had] little or nothing to say in her own behalf, only seemed to rely on what the court should do, and thereupon consented to be tried in the water and likewise to be searched again...."

On the morning of July 10, 1706, Grace was moved to Old Donation Church. There, she was allowed to do penance and was searched by a group of older women to make sure she had no amulets or herbs on her person that might assist her to escape.

She was then loaded on a wagon and taken down a dirt road to Lynnhaven Bay, on a point of land where county citizens had assembled to observe her ducking. To this day, the avenue traveled by Grace and the sheriff bears the name "Witchduck Road," and the area where Grace's neighbors gathered is known as "Witchduck Point."

The avowed sorceress was led down a narrow path to the water's edge, where, with the exception of a petticoat, she was stripped of her clothing and bound.

Oral tradition claims that Grace proved to be as slippery as an eel, and the sheriff and his deputies struggled unsuccessfully to tie her up. Finally, a bystander suggested that a Bible be tied around her neck, and once that was accomplished, the story claims, Grace immediately ceased to resist.

According to the literature I reviewed, people traveled from great distances to view the water test. Supposedly, it was a beautiful day, warm and with a cloudless, deep blue sky arching overhead.

As the sheriff was about to load Grace into the boat, the legend claims, she turned her face to the crowd of onlookers and shouted,

"You poor, white-trash hypocrites. You've come from hither and yon to see me get ducked, but before you get home, you will get the ducking of your lives!"

Grace was then rowed out to deep water and lowered overboard, with care taken to ensure her safety. To the dismay of court officials, she somehow managed to remain afloat.

The accused witch was brought ashore and searched again by a group of elderly women, who reported that they found two black marks, the same that Elizabeth Barnes had cited earlier.

The official record reads: "She [Grace Sherwood] swam...and afterwards being searched by five ancient women, who have all declared on oath that she is not like them nor other women that they knew, having two things like tits on her private parts of a black color, being blacker than the rest of her body, all which circumstance the court weighting [sic] in their consideration do therefore order that the sheriff take the said Grace into his custody and to commit her body to the common goal [sic—jail] of this county, there to secure her by irons, or otherwise there to remain till such time as [she is] brought to a future trial."

After Grace was ducked, popular folklore claims that a sudden and ominous stillness settled over all of Princess Anne County and Lynnhaven Bay, and a crescendo of thunder from the darkening sky nearly deafened the dispersing crowd. People ran for cover in panic as a torrential downpour enveloped them. Almost instantly the land is said to have flooded, and those who had come to witness the ducking were washed into ditches and swept along into Lynnhaven Bay. Grace's prophecy had come to pass, and the wild shrieks of her mocking laughter could allegedly be heard above the chaos and roar of the storm. None of this, of course, is mentioned in the court records.

One folktale informs us that the sheriff was unable to keep Grace in jail while she was awaiting trial for witchcraft. The devil, it claims, would appear each night and unlock his minion's fetters. Together, the pair would fly to a point of land jutting into Lynnhaven Bay, there to dance the night away. With the crowing of the cock at dawn, the devil always returned Grace to her cell, where she slept the day away. No vegetation, the legend insists, has ever again grown on the spot where the couple danced.

In another story, Grace is said to have asked the sheriff if he would like to see something he had never seen before and would never see again. Out of curiosity he consented to his prisoner's offer, and Grace instructed a young boy to go to the local tavern and fetch her two pewter plates that had never been washed.

The boy went to the tavern, but disobeyed his instructions and rinsed the plates in a rain barrel and carefully dried them.

Grace could not be fooled. Taking the pewter plates from the boy, she banged them on his head and instructed him to return to the tavern for two more. "And don't dip them in the rain barrel this time," she shouted after him.

When the boy returned with two new and unwashed plates, Grace talked the sheriff into releasing her from her cell so she could perform the demonstration. As soon as she was clear of the prison walls, Grace is said to have clapped a plate under each of her arms and quickly flew away.

The laws of Virginia in the seventeenth century enumerated witchcraft as a felony without benefit of clergy, which meant that it was a capital offense. Capital offenses were tried in the General Court, located in Williamsburg, and if found guilty, a plaintiff faced execution by hanging.

I have read that officials anxiously labored over the accusations made against Grace, hesitant to proceed with her case for two reasons: The charges were not specifically supported, and prosecutors feared the possibility of initiating a witch craze like the one that had devastated Salem, Massachusetts.

Unfortunately, we do not know what happened to Grace between 1707 and 1714. One historian simply states that the record is silent about any future action against her. Another writes that general court documents for the period have been lost, claiming that when the Virginia government moved from Williamsburg to Richmond, records were collected there and later destroyed in a fire in 1865, when the capitol fell to Union forces in the Civil War. That writer believes that the early chronicles of Princess Anne survived only because the clerk of the county court did not trust state officials, and, rather than forward his logs, he buried them in his backyard. I have made no attempt to verify or disprove either of these claims.

On June 16, 1714, surviving records show that Grace agreed to pay a sum of two pounds of tobacco per acre for back taxes on the hundred and forty-five acres of land that her father had bequeathed to her and which had reverted to the state. Some believe this document is evidence that Grace was imprisoned for the seven years following her ducking.

Life apparently became more stable for Grace Sherwood thereafter, as her name does not appear again in county records until her death, twenty-six years later, in 1740. Her will, in which she devised her property to her three sons, John, James and Richard, was probated on the first day of October. John was named executor.

The court recorded an inventory of Grace's personal property on December 3, listing her possessions as five head of cattle (one four-year-old steer, one three-year-old steer, one three-year-old heifer and two, two-year-old heifers), one hand mill, one frame table with draw, one chest, one box, one iron spit, three low chairs, one English blanket, one iron pot, a pewter dish and a basin, evidence of a sparse lifestyle but not unusual for the times.

Even in death, Grace's legend continued to grow. Supposedly she enjoyed sitting near the fireplace in her declining years, her feet propped up to its warmth. Finally, as the hour of her death approached, a great storm raged outside and Grace asked to be moved closer to the glowing coals so she might warm her feet one last time.

As she lay there, a whirling gust of wind descended through the chimney, causing ashes from the fireplace to cloud the room. When the dust settled, Grace was gone, and inscribed in soot at the base of the fireplace was a hoof print. The devil had come to claim his own.

Another story would have us believe that on the morning when Pungo Township's witch was laid to rest, it began to rain and continued for seven days and seven nights, and on the eighth dawn her casket bobbed to the surface. Grace's sons retrieved the body, bailed floodwaters from the grave and reburied their mother, only to have a second cloudburst drench the land and again set the coffin adrift.

A passing neighbor reported that he saw a black cat sitting on the disinterred casket, and word that Grace had arisen quickly spread throughout the community. Some township residents, the legend indicates, became so frightened that they immediately left the region, abandoning their possessions.

As her weary sons buried Grace once more, a call to arms went out, and the remaining men of Pungo banded together to hunt down and shoot every cat that could be found.

Perhaps there is a grain of truth to the legend, for in 1743, three years after Grace's death, Pungo Township is reported to have suffered a severe infestation of rats and mice, supposedly brought on by a shortage of cats.

In Grace Sherwood's time and throughout history as well, women have been the primary objects of witch fears and have been much more likely than men to face formal charges. There has usually been an erotic dimension attributed to witches. They have been viewed as lewd, wanton seductresses, controlled by unrestrained lust. Grace's beauty was surely envied by women and a temptation to men.

We have observed that Grace wore men's clothing. A modern male would not normally consider such attire to be sexually stimulating, but we need to remember that colonial dress was designed to hide a woman's figure. The sparser, trimmer garments of men, I am sure, displayed her figure to far more advantage than the billowing layers of women's garb.

And then there were the "two marks on her private parts." Witches were believed to have additional teats at locations where women experienced their greatest erotic pleasures, and on these the devil and familiars were believed to suckle. It seems obvious to us now that Grace had several moles on her body. A modern physician would caution her to be alert for changes in color and size, which might signal the development of skin cancer.

Like so many other poor souls who have been accused of witchcraft through the ages, Grace Sherwood's only "crime" was probably a desire to live an independent life.

Grace was buried near a large tree that I am told remains standing to this day. On evenings when the moon rises full, cats are said to come from near and far to sit in its branches and yowl, and as the feline chorus overwhelms the lesser strains of night, the Witch of Pungo arises and joins in the serenade.

Patricia Pigg, a Distant Cousin of Joe Johnson, Photographs
"Patty Cannon's House"

Patty Cannon's House

In the northwest quadrant of the offset crossroads that mark the village of Reliance in Dorchester County, Maryland—literally a stone's throw from the Mason-Dixon Line—stands a tidy frame house that closely resembles many other dwellings scattered throughout the Delmarva Peninsula. Photographs of the structure taken prior to renovations and the construction of an addition in the 1970s display an even less remarkable façade.

Just outside the front-yard boundary, however, a cast-iron marker erected by the Maryland State Roads Commission informs passers-by that the property's history is anything but commonplace:

PATTY CANNON'S HOUSE
AT JOHNSON'S CROSS ROADS WHERE
THE NOTED KIDNAPPING GROUP HAD
HEADQUARTERS AS DESCRIBED IN
GEORGE ALFRED TOWNSEND'S NOVEL
"THE ENTAILED HAT." THE HOUSE
BORDERS ON CAROLINE AND DOR-
CHESTER COUNTIES AND THE STATE
OF DELAWARE.

Tourists and natives alike stop to gawk and take photographs, and a few knock on Jack and Rose Messick's door to inquire about Patty and the "dungeon in the attic," where the gang is alleged to have chained captives until they could be transported to southern ports and sold into slavery.

For the benefit of those readers who did not grow up in lower Delaware or on the Eastern Shore of Maryland, where children were once disciplined with threats of Patty Cannon and where her legend has been perpetuated and embellished for nearly two centuries, a few words of background are in order.

As plantation agriculture spread westward into the newly formed Gulf States during the early years of the nineteenth century, the demand for manual labor increased and prices for quality slaves reached record highs—sometimes exceeding a thousand dollars for young, strong individuals. While the Underground Railway clandestinely conveyed escaped slaves north to freedom, kidnappers, including Patty and Jesse Cannon and a succession of acquaintances and in-laws, were engaged in the lucrative criminal practice of conveying *free* blacks in the opposite direction into bondage.

Eventually, after the death of Jesse and under mounting pressure from officials in several states, surviving members of the family escaped prosecution by moving south and then west into Texas. Patty remained behind and was eventually apprehended. She died in a Delaware jail in 1829 while under indictment for several murders that were never tried.

Two properties in the town of Reliance were once associated with the Cannons and Joe Johnson, their son-in-law. The long-time residence of Patty and Jesse, a few hundred yards from the state boundary in Sussex County, Delaware, was situated on one of them. The second is the lot in Dorchester County that was purchased by Johnson in 1821 and sold to Patty in 1826, on which the Messick house now stands.

Unfortunately, Patty Cannon's biographers have been novelists rather than historians, and that circumstance raises a severe challenge to those who now attempt to clarify even the simplest facts about her life. The two works of fiction that have most influenced the Cannon-Johnson legend are the *Narrative and Confessions of Lucretia Cannon, the Female Murderer*, written by an anonymous author, and *The Entailed Hat*, penned by the popular and prolific eighteenth-century journalist George Alfred Townsend or "GATH," as he often signed his work.

The *Narrative* is a twenty-three-page Gothic horror tale published in 1841, twelve years after Patty's death. Although it is blatantly inaccurate in nearly every detail, including Patty's given name, it has shaped almost everything written about her life for more than a century and a half.

On the other hand, *The Entailed Hat* is a complex, five-hundred-and-sixty-five page novel containing some legitimate historical events and figures (though often realigned by Townsend to make his story work) as well as a considerable amount of fiction. Since its publication in 1884, however, many readers have accepted the entire story as legitimate history.

The inaccuracies in these two volumes, along with a vast array of local and regional folklore, have been so frequently repeated and so widely distributed that no effort to discern the truth will ever be sufficient to overcome the misinformation that continues to proliferate. Let me cite just one example of the liberties that writers have taken over the years.

Patty was indicted in 1829 for strangling a female infant and participating with others in the murder of a male child in 1822, as well as the undated killings of an unknown male and an African American boy. Each of the four charges was supported by the testimony of a single individual, a young man that Patty had raised, and, as noted earlier, none of the allegations were ever tried in a court of law.

Twelve years later, however, the *Narrative and Confessions* informed its readers that Patty had committed eleven murders and was involved in more than a dozen others. By 1997, one journalist had upped the total of Patty's personally committed homicides to twenty and accused her of assisting in at least twenty others, and recently I read that more than thirty died by her own hand.

Because the avenues of interest surrounding Patty Cannon are too numerous and complicated to all be addressed in a single article, our focus on these pages will be restricted to a brief examination of Patty's house, or, I should say, of Patty's two houses, and to a pair of questions that especially intrigues us: (1) Did Patty Cannon and Joe Johnson operate a tavern in Reliance? (2) Is the house that stands today on the northwest corner where Maryland Route 577 meets Route 392 the building in which Patty lived between 1826 and her death in 1829?

The *Narrative* informs us that Patty and Jesse (whom it calls "Lucretia" and "Alonzo," respectively) settled on the Nanticoke River and founded Cannon's Ferry. Then, after poisoning Jesse, the tale continues, Patty moved to Johnson's Cross Roads where she established a "low tavern" in which to carry on her nefarious activities.

Pure rubbish! Cannon's Ferry (now Woodland) was established long before Patty and Jesse's time by another branch of the Cannon family. The only documented home in which Patty and Jesse lived together was in Reliance (first named Wilson's Cross Roads and later Johnson's Cross Roads), and all contemporary references to the structure call it a house, never a tavern. As described earlier, the building stood in Sussex County, a few hundred yards from the historical marker and the Messick home. The present property owners claim it was dismantled in 1948.

A newspaper article in the *Easton Gazette*, dated July 23, 1821, tells of the arrest of Joe Johnson at the Cannon residence on July 14 of that year. The italics and parenthesis in the four following paragraphs are mine.

"On Monday morning about 10 o'clock, Miles Tindall and Purnell Johnson, two deputy sheriffs, with two or three constables and several other inhabitants of that County (Sussex), went to *the house* of Jesse Cannon, situate in North West Fork Hundred, within a few hundred yards of the Maryland line, to execute their writs (against Jesse Cannon, Joseph Johnson and others for the recovery of three kidnapped victims). There they found Johnson and Cannon.

"At first Johnson threatened to shoot any person who should attempt to enter *the house*, or to arrest him. After a little parley, Johnson, finding that the officers were determined at all risks to have him, surrendered.

"*The house* was opened, and after securing Johnson, they searched for the three negroes mentioned in the writs of replevy.

"They found the negroes and ten others, all confined in *the house* and some of them in irons, waiting the arrival of a vessel for transporting them to some of the Southern states."

On the day that Johnson was arrested, he had negotiated the purchase of one hundred and sixteen square perches (about three-quarters of an acre) in the corner where Dorchester County meets Caroline and Sussex Counties, the land on which the Messick house now stands. The deed fails to state whether the property then contained any improvements.

Local folklore and *The Entailed Hat* (the former often generated by the latter) claim that Johnson built a tavern on this property, and that it became the headquarters for a band of cutthroats led by Patty and Joe and a character named Van Dorn. The novel contains the detailed story of a raid on the Cowgill House, now Woodburn, the Delaware governor's mansion in Dover. During the foray, Van Dorn is accidentally and mortally wounded by one of his men, later to die in "Johnson's tavern" in the arms of Patty.

Both Van Dorn's character and the raid on Dover, however, were created by the fertile mind of GATH for the purpose of making his story better, and one has to wonder if all the popular lore about local citizens stopping at the tavern to have a drink with Patty Cannon was not created in the fertile minds of our grandfathers for the same reason. Delmarvians are famous for having paved a wonderful legacy of tall tales and legends, and many generations have now had an opportunity to practice on Patty.

John M. Clayton, attorney, judge, Delaware Secretary of State, United States Senator and Secretary of State under President Taylor, was a man who knew the Cannons and Johnsons and who personally prosecuted Joe Johnson in 1822. In his papers and letters, Clayton refers to "Johnson's house" and "Cannon's house," never to a tavern.

In *The History of Seaford* (written during the 1890s), which, admittedly, is not always accurate, Robert B. Hazzard mentioned Joe and Patty's houses in these words (the italics and parenthesis are mine): "She (Patty) formed an alliance in the business of buying and stealing negroes with Joe Johnson, who married one of her daughters (she only had one) and made his residence in the large two storied and attic *house* which then and for many years *stood* at Johnson's Crossroads, now Reliance, where the beautiful home of W. Matthew Smith (the current Messick house) now stands. She had for her home the small farm and *house* which is still standing and occupied as a home in the field nearly opposite the Gethsemane M. P. Church on the north side of the county road."

Once again, the word "house" is used when referring to both properties, and Hazzard employs the past tense when referring to Joe's home in 1890. We know that major renovations or new construction occurred on the lot prior to its ownership by the Smith family, but the details are not clear.

But let us put aside all evidence to the contrary for a moment and assume that Joe Johnson did build a tavern on the Reliance site, and that it served as a kidnapping headquarters for Johnson and Cannon during the last few years of their operation in the 1820s.

I have recognized that Townsend was a very capable journalist, and his descriptions of historical sites and buildings in his novel are very detailed. Take a copy of *The Entailed Hat* to Woodburn in Dover or to the Teackle Mansion in Princess Anne, for example, and compare the pictures he painted in words to these surviving structures. You will be amazed at how accurately Townsend portrayed them. Then go to Reliance and apply the same test to his characterization of "Joe Johnson's Tavern." You will find no similarities to the Messick house.

We will probably never know with certainty whether the land Wilson sold to Johnson contained a building or whether Joe later put one there. We do know that he spent considerable time away from the crossroads between the date he purchased the property and its subsequent sale to Patty Cannon in 1826, when he fled from Delmarva with his family and Patty moved across the line into Maryland.

As reported earlier, Joe was arrested in the Cannon residence in 1821 and removed to the Georgetown Jail, where he was tried in 1822, found guilty of kidnapping and flogged at Delaware's infamous "Red Hannah," the jail's whipping post. Thereafter, records show that he frequently occupied himself by sailing his schooner to Philadelphia, where he supervised the kidnapping of young blacks, whom he then removed to southern states and sold into slavery. With such a busy schedule, one has to wonder where he would have found the spare time to build and manage a tavern.

In summary, I have seen nothing written before *The Entailed Hat* was published—fifty-five years after Patty's death—that mentions a Johnson or Cannon tavern. In none of the contemporary documents, which include depositions, articles in Delaware, Pennsylvania and Maryland newspapers, as well as numerous letters, is there any allusion to a tavern when referring to the Cannon or Johnson houses. I find it difficult, therefore, to disagree with Sharon Moore, who has researched the Cannons and Johnsons over a period of many years, when she says, "I don't believe Joe Johnson had a tavern until George Alfred Townsend gave him one in *The Entailed Hat*, and everything written after its publication has been polluted with legend over fact."

Patty Cannon
and the
History Detectives

I t is well known on Maryland's Eastern Shore and throughout Delaware that a group operating from the border town of Reliance in the first quarter of the nineteenth century was engaged in kidnapping free African Americans and selling them into slavery in the South. Tradition informs us that a woman called Patty Cannon led this assortment of cutthroats, but the bulk of Patty's biographers have been novelists rather than historians, an unfortunate circumstance that has produced volumes of fabrication and folklore, upon which journalists have eagerly fed for nearly two centuries. Isolating the truth about this woman of mystery is now a difficult task.

I was pleased, therefore, when an executive from Lion Television in New York called to say he was producing a segment about Patty Cannon for the PBS *History Detectives* series and wanted to learn the facts behind the legend. His primary interest was to determine whether the house belonging to Jack and Rose Messick in Reliance, which a historical marker identifies as "Patty Cannon's House," was the real thing.

At the end of the show's premiere, while credits were still rolling on television screens across America, my telephone rang. The gentleman caller could not wait to express his indignation with certain conclusions reached by the "detectives," and since then I have listened to a variety of concerns about the documentary. While not all of the discontent is justified, several unfortunate errors have reduced the informed audience's enthusiasm and confidence in this otherwise interesting and worthwhile series.

Gwendolyn Wright, a professor of architectural history at Columbia University and one of four "detectives," comments as she reads the original deed registrations that conveyed what is now the Messick property to Joe Johnson in 1821 and then to Patty Cannon in 1826: "It's significant that there's no mention of a house on the land, which strengthens my belief that the Messick's house must have been built after Patty's time."

While the visible elements of the Messick structure clearly do not date to the first quarter of the nineteenth century, there is absolutely no significance to the fact that Patty's deed failed to mention a house. The purpose of a deed is to affect the conveyance of land, and it is rare for one to contain details of property improvements.

Wright then discovers a 1968 newspaper article that mentions the house where Patty and her husband, Jesse, had lived in Sussex County, and from it she concludes that Patty never lived in Dorchester. "So this was not Patty Cannon's house, definitively!" she says of the Messick home.

How disappointing that a member of the academic community would accept a newspaper article written more than a hundred and forty years after the fact as a primary source of evidence and look no farther for the truth. It is even more baffling to realize that Wright apparently failed to read the entire article, as it contradicts at least part of her conclusion.

Wright voices, yet fails to heed an important clue to suggest that a house *was* built on the lot after Joe Johnson purchased it and before he sold it to Patty and fled to Florida in 1826. Johnson's cost for less than an acre of land at Wilson's Cross Roads was $150, yet Patty paid $1,000 for it five years later. A small parcel of land in a remote region on Maryland's Eastern Shore in those days did not appreciate by 667% in five years unless something had been added to it.

But we need not depend entirely upon common sense to support the fact that a house existed on Johnson's land at the crossroads, and that both he and Patty lived there.

Dorchester County land records dated November 12, 1822, inform us that Joseph Johnson moved from Sussex County to Dorchester County on October 18, 1822, and community history and tradition agree that he set up housekeeping with his family on the same three quarters of an acre where the Messicks now live.

The first proof we have of Patty's residency on the Messick property is her arrest in August 1827 by Dorchester County Sheriff (later Maryland Governor) Thomas Holiday Hicks. Jacob Cannon, a distant cousin to her late husband and the individual from whom the couple had rented their Sussex County home, sued Patty for an unpaid debt. Dorchester neighbor Ezekial Wheatley posted her bail, and litigation of the case dragged on for nearly two years.

Patty was scheduled for a court hearing in Cambridge on April 2, 1829, but human remains were discovered the day before on the farm she formerly rented across the road in Delaware, and she was taken into custody by Sussex County authorities.

While Patty sat in the Georgetown Jail on April 6, a Dorchester judge ruled on the lawsuit in favor of the plaintiff, Jacob Cannon. Orders were issued to confiscate the property that now belongs to the Messicks, and Patty's lot and house were sold at public auction in October—after Patty had died—to General Jesse Green of Concord, Delaware.

Contemporary newspaper articles about Patty's arrest in 1829 provide additional evidence of her residency on the Maryland side of the crossroads.

Through land records, we are able to identify most of the families that have lived on the Messick property since the hated woman's demise. Interestingly, one early resident of Patty's house was the son of the deputy who transported her to prison.

But it is legitimate to question whether the building that stands on the property today is the same one that Joe and Patty called home?

In Scharf's *History of Delaware*, its author indicates that the original house was remodeled by Charles M. Phillips, a Reliance postmaster, in 1885; and the same newspaper article that Wright displays on the show informs us that the old structure "was rebuilt in such a way that virtually nothing from the old tavern remained."

There are numerous other references to indicate that Patty's Dorchester home no longer survives, at least not in its entirety or its original form. Whether it was ever a tavern is another debate. Major renovation again occurred during the twentieth century, and an addition has also been constructed.

Whether any of the Messick house contains timbers from the structure that Patty Cannon once called home, or how much it may contain, are not easy puzzles to solve. Dismantling the building may be the only way to arrive at an informed judgment, and Jack and Rose Messick are not *that* interested in knowing the whole truth.

In any event, I must take strong exception to Wright's suggestion that the Maryland Roads Commission was being deceitful when it erected the marker that stands on the edge of what is a genuine historic property.

Carol Wilson, professor of history at Maryland's Washington College, was retained by the producer to document Patty as a legitimate historical figure and contributed the other errors that need to be addressed. At one point in Wilson's narrative, with her hand resting on a copy of the contemporary *African Observer* magazine, she makes the following comment: "Peter Hook later says, 'We were severely whipped by Johnson for saying that we were free,' and even says in his deposition here that he once heard Johnson's wife—that's Patty Cannon's daughter—declare that it did her good to see him beat the boys."

There are two problems with Wilson's statement. The first part of her sentence—the reference to being beaten for claiming to be free—does appear in the testimony of Peter Hook, but the second part—the reference to Johnson's wife—is found in the testimony of a different victim named Samuel Scomp. And if we examine a little more of Scomp's statement, another error by Wilson becomes apparent. "Within 7 miles of Rocky Spring, Joe Johnson, one of the boys, died in the wagon in consequence of the frequent beatings he received from Ebenezer Johnson; deponent once heard Johnson's wife declare that it did her good to see him beat the boys...."

There is no misprint on the part of the *African Observer*. Joe Johnson was the name of one of the free black boys kidnapped in Philadelphia and shipped south in 1825. The error is that Ebenezer Johnson was married to Sally Shehee, and it is Sally whom Scomp quotes. Patty's daughter, Mary, was married to Ebenezer's brother, Joe.

Some viewers of the show have raised concern that Elyse Luray, an auctioneer and appraiser and another of the four "detectives" who investigate and narrate the series, makes the observation that Patty died in prison of "natural causes," but Luray may be correct.

The bulk of tradition, of course, claims that Patty poisoned herself, while a few hold to the belief that she was murdered and a very small number to an idea that she was spirited from prison and migrated to Canada or the American West.

The truth is that we have discovered no records thus far that officially document the cause of her death, and Patty was a woman in her sixties, old for that period in our history. It is just my personal feeling, but if she had committed suicide, I think the newspapers would have said so, rather than simply report as they did: "She died in jail on the 11th instant."

Men and women write and speak our news, our history and our television shows, and men and women will forever be fallible, myself very much included. We can only hope that every possible effort is made to write and speak the truth. In the case of Patty Cannon and the History Detectives, that effort regrettably fell a little short.

Only Haunted People

Man has probably debated the existence of ghosts since Neanderthals huddled around their campfires 200,000 years ago. Our art and literature stand replete with sometimes benign and often horrific tales and illustrations of spirits that survived beyond the grave, and recently we have experienced a proliferation of photographic "evidence" to "support" their existence. Everyone, it seems, is taking pictures of ghosts these days, and the most common manifestations are generally referred to as "orbs."

What, exactly, are these typically fuzzy globes that have suddenly populated our earth in such staggering numbers? Why do they only appear in photographs or to the naked eyes of a chosen few? Where have they been throughout most of our history? I posed the following question to a popular Internet ghost-hunting group: "Can someone explain to me, please, precisely what an orb is?"

The reply came quickly: "An orb is a human spirit, deceased, that has taken on the form of a round sphere of light. It appears to have 'light' as its main composition due to the fact that they are reflective and are better photographed under dark or dim lighting conditions."

"I have difficulty understanding," I wrote again, "how so many untrained photographers with inexpensive cameras manage to capture images of them, when I have never seen a single one on the thousands of photographs I have taken, nor have several professional friends who have made literally hundreds of thousands of photographs in their careers. How can I explain that?"

To my second question I received two replies: "Quite often when the photos are being developed, the developers will crop out the orbs, thinking they are a defective portion of the photo," the first began. "They are trying to help, but not when that's what you're shooting for. (lol) When you take the pics in, tell them NO changes, that you want them AS IS! Have you tried taking pics in notably haunted locations or cemeteries?"

Knowing from considerable experience that you can't get the typical photo processor to crop a picture even if you beg, I was somewhat confused by the answer.

The second reply was even more bewildering: "This may be simply explained by the fact that most people have the photo companies give them photos that 'they' believe to be good. As far as professional photographers? This may be the 'photo isn't right' syndrome here too. They look like bad photos."

"What makes it possible," I began an exchange with another, hopefully more informed group, "to take a picture of a ghost that the human eye can't see?"

"That's easy," came the reply. "The eye can only see what the light shows it, and it's changing all the time. The eye can't see the spectrum of light where the ghost is, but the camera can freeze a tiny fraction of a second and capture it all on film or on a disk. It can see all the spectrums. Many people believe that spirits move too fast for the eye to see them."

"I have to tell you that I'm skeptical about that," I responded.

"It's good to be skeptical. If you're skeptical, you want to believe. You just need some evidence. Non-believers are something else. It doesn't matter what you show them, they aren't capable of understanding the facts. They don't want to. They just don't care."

"But," I tried to define my skepticism, "I can clearly see a racing car or a horse or a man running, while to the average camera that people use to take ghost photographs, those things would be nothing more than a blur, unless you moved the camera at the same speed they were moving, and then the background would be blurred."

"I think you're a non-believer instead of a skeptic. I can see it's not going to matter what evidence I give you."

"I think the questions are fair. How can we resolve people's reservations and questions if we can't discuss them?"

"You need to do some reading and talk to more people. Then maybe you'll understand what I'm telling you."

More "evidence" in the form of descriptive and interpretive literature about orbs and more alleged personal contacts with them are to be found on the Internet than you may ever have the time to contemplate in your lifetime. In addition, thousands of photographs of these ethereal objects have been posted there.

I should clarify that the word "orb" has no specific historical association with anything supernatural, having its roots in the Latin "orbis" and the Middle English "orbe," which refer to a circle or something circular. The Paranormal Research Society of Texas appears to have been the first to impart a ghostly connotation to the term.

The PRST lays claim to having coined the term "ghost (or spirit) orb" in 1996 when members began to photograph spheres of light with the newly developed digital camera. It is no surprise, then, that the society has much to say about orbs.

"We created the Orb Theory based on the findings of our field investigations and our research. We discovered that an orb represented the soul of a departed person, the soul being the essence of who they were in life, complete with their intelligence, their emotions and their personality. [The PRST does not say *how* this was discovered.] The orb or sphere is common in our everyday lives. The earth and moon are spheres. Our blood cells are sphere shaped. The vision of Black Elk describes hoops within hoops. We use the symbol of the circle to represent eternal existence with no beginning or end.

"We teach that a spirit is represented in an orb configuration pattern. When the spirit is moving about, its shape is an orb, but when it comes to rest, meaning that it is no longer in motion, the spirit energy that is compressed within the orb is released and this spirit energy expands into what we call Ecto-Vapor or Ectoplasm. Often an orb will contain more than one soul, and when its spirit energy is released, multiple orbs flow forth from the single orb."

The view that such an apparition is an actual soul and that it contains the intelligence, emotions and personality of a departed human appears to be widely held. This "life force," believers will tell you, survives death because it is made of energy, and energy cannot be destroyed.

"When we're alive, we're made of energy. The body is just the shell that the energy rides around in. The energy is what we really are. Science has proved that you can't destroy energy, so when you die, all the energy goes out into the atmosphere. But it usually doesn't go very far, and it just goes on doing the things it did in life.

"You talk to a lot of medical people and they'll tell you that when somebody dies, there's like a flash around their head. [Ten doctors and nurses I asked have never witnessed nor heard of this phenomenon.] That's the energy leaving the body. That's what a ghost is. We've got a lot of ghosts around who don't realize they're dead."

Some experienced ghost hunters believe that the best times to take photographs of ghosts are periods of increased solar flare activity, when magnetic fields are expanded. Since electromagnetic force meters spike in the presence of a ghost, they contend, it proves that ghosts are a form of energy. The more electromagnetic forces there are in the atmosphere, the more fuel they have to manifest themselves as apparitions.

I was told that it takes a tremendous amount of energy for a spirit to materialize. "Ghosts are well known to drain batteries from the cameras, flashlights, recorders and cars of people trying to record them."

Some believe that castles and old buildings in Europe produce more visible manifestations of ghosts because the stone used to manufacture them is magnetic. Since older cemeteries in the United States are said to produce the most photographic anomalies, these theorists speculate that older headstones also possess a higher magnetic quality.

"O.K., assuming that a ghost is a magnetic energy field, why do most appear as orbs?" I inquired of a believer.

"They can take any shape they want," my correspondent replied, "but an orb is the most simple form to attain. They use that shape when they move about because it's easier."

"The orb is the basic energy pattern of the spirit world," I was informed by a member of another paranormal investigation group. "Since orbs are the most common shapes that ghosts take, you expect to see them everywhere, and if you're receptive, you do."

"Exactly what does it mean to be receptive?" I inquired.

"The ghosts are the ones that decide whether or not they want to be photographed, so when you get one in a picture, it's the result of their willing it. Some people can experience paranormal phenomena and some can't. The ones that do can also pick up things on film that others don't."

"Does that mean," I countered, ignoring the fact that my question had been ignored, "that if a skeptic who has never seen a ghost stands side-by-side with an experienced ghost hunter and photographs the same scene, the believer's camera will record any ghosts that are present and the skeptic's will not?"

"Most of the time that is correct."

"Then why do so many people who are non-believers take pictures and find orbs in them?"

"That would be because the spirits have decided to allow themselves to be photographed. When, how or why they choose to appear is their doing. They might allow you to photograph them, but if you're not a believer, it's doubtful that they would.

"And keep something in mind if you try it," my advisor continued; "you should never take spirit pictures in a group. Spirits will pick up the vibes of those around you, and you don't want to be held accountable for the feelings of others."

"One reason that most scientific investigators fail to come up with evidence of ghosts," another ghost chaser claimed, "is because they lack understanding and respect for the spirits of the dead. They do not understand that ghosts have intelligence, attitudes, feelings and emotions. What ghost in his or her right mind would want to deal with such a person? Would you?

"If you conduct an investigation with your mind full of doubt, the doubts will project themselves—thoughts are energy too—and the spirit will have no interest in showing itself or communicating with you. People trained in ghost hunting are able to capture so many orbs with their cameras because they know how to act around ghosts. They treat the ghosts with respect. They talk to them and get their permission to take photographs. If you treat them like you treat your friends, they will reveal themselves and will even talk to you."

"I always ask the ghost permission to take a picture," a member of the Maryland Ghost and Spirit Association related. "I forgot one time at Pretty Boy Dam and the whole roll of film did not come out."

Once you are in the correct frame of mind to approach and communicate with ghosts, the International Ghost Hunters' Society recommends that you use a digital camera to take your pictures. Since this new technology became available a few years ago, hundreds of thousands of "ghost" photographs have been taken around the world.

Before we examine why the digital camera is such a powerful device for recording "ghosts," allow me to briefly review a little of the history of spirit photography.

Photography capable of producing a permanent image began in 1839 with the Daguerreotype and became an instant success. People everywhere flocked to studios to have their likeness preserved.

The early cameras required a subject to sit motionless for a full minute or longer with the lens open. If the sitter moved while the lens was ajar, a double image was recorded on the sensitized plate. Another figure could be introduced into the setting during the procedure or a second, double exposure could be made. The shorter the exposure time, the fainter the image would be.

The first man to take advantage of these anomalies for profit and fame appears to have been a Boston-based photographer by the name of William H. Mumler. In 1861, Mumler began offering séance photo sessions. While subjects were being photographed, the photographer's assistant, dressed in a cloak or robe, would sneak into the scene behind the subject, remain for ten or twenty seconds and then leave. When the picture was developed, a semi-transparent apparition would be present on the plate.

Mumler was exposed in court as a fake in 1872, but not before he had collected a tidy sum of money with his chicanery. By the 1890s, spirit photography had become a fad, and using a camera to communicate with spirits (or using the camera to allow spirits to communicate with you, as I was recently corrected) continues as a form of mediumship today.

The International Ghost Hunters' Society, which has brought a degree of fame and fortune to its founder, Dave Oster, strongly advocates the digital camera for capturing ghost orbs. According to Oster, spirits can better enable a digital camera to capture their images because they, like the camera, are electromagnetic in nature.

"And when you see those little blobs of light in the pictures you take around the house," one ghost buster admonishes, "don't cut it out. Enlarge it and frame it and put it with your family photographs. It's probably your Aunt Agnes!"

A woman who is firmly convinced that orbs appearing in photographs are the spirits of departed humans referred me to Galileo Galilei (1564-1642), the Italian astronomer, philosopher, mathematician and inventor who is probably best remembered by the average student of science for his experiments at the leaning Tower of Pisa, in which he demonstrated that bodies of different weights fall at the same velocity.

Galileo was also an early believer in the Copernican theory—that the earth and other planets revolve around the sun—but publicly avoided the subject for many years to avoid risking the Vatican's ire. His development of a telescope with 32X magnification eventually contributed to confirmation of the theory.

In 1611, Galileo visited Rome and demonstrated the wonders of his invention. Encouraged by a generally warm reception, he finally ventured, in 1613, to issue a strong position on the workings of our solar system, thus drawing the attention of church authorities to differences between the new scientific view and certain passages in the scriptures. Outrage from church authorities resulted in an admonishment by Pope Paul V not to "hold, teach or defend" the heretical and condemned Copernican doctrine.

Galileo fell silent, but after years in studious retirement, he published the results of his continued thought and investigation. In spite of acclaim from scholars across Europe, the church banned his new book, and its author was censured and ordered to Rome to stand before the Inquisition under menace of torture. Galileo recanted and spent the rest of his life in strict seclusion.

But what, you are surely asking, is Galileo's connection to ghost orbs?

A story is told that when he took his telescope to Rome and asked church officials to look through it and observe its revelations, the cardinals refused. My correspondent declares that those who question the validity of ghost orbs are no different than the cardinals—they are refusing to look at the evidence.

I cannot resist citing a passage from St. Matthew that I believe may apply equally to the cardinals and to my correspondent: "And if the blind lead the blind, both shall fall into the ditch."

The International Ghost Hunters Society was the first national ghost hunting organization to take a strong position on incorporating digital cameras into field investigations of the supernatural and, like the correspondent above, many of its members are critical of all who raise questions about the validity of "ghost" photographs taken with this relatively new technology.

Even though camera manufacturers are among those who offer research-supported explanations for the orbs that appear in photos, one spokesman informed me that the logic of critics is flawed.

"The critics suggest all kinds of lame excuses why digital imaging is not practical or reliable, but the digital camera has been proven time and again to be very reliable and effective at capturing ghostly anomalies. We have thousands of photographs obtained with a multitude of different digital cameras posted on the Ghost Web, proving that the digital camera is an excellent ghost-hunting tool."

In order to continue toward an informed judgment, you need to understand two primary facts about orb photographs: (1) They were very rare before the advent of compact, affordable digital cameras. (2) They are almost always flash photographs.

Since digital cameras have produced most of the orb photos, it is demonstrably true that digital cameras are superior for orb photography. But why is this so?

The Fujifilm Corporation, a major manufacturer of photography products, has received so many inquiries about orbs and other anomalies in photographs that they have initiated a web page to explain them.

When you take pictures using the flash, whitish round dots appear in various parts of the image.

There is always a certain amount of dust floating around in the air. You may have noticed this at the movies when you look up at the light coming from the movie projector and notice the bright sparks floating around in the beam.

In the same way, there are always dust particles floating around nearby when you take pictures with your camera.

When you use the flash, the light from the flash reflects off the dust particles and is sometimes captured in your shot.

Of course, dust particles very close to the camera are blurred since they are not in focus, but because they reflect the light more strongly than the more distant main subject of the shot, that reflected light can sometimes be captured by the camera and recorded on the resulting image as round white spots. So these dots are the blurred images of dust particles.

You can reproduce this problem relatively easily by taking a picture right after you put away goods that create a lot of dust, such as feather bedding.

In actual photography, this problem frequently arises in shots taken at construction sites, etc. It may also occur when it is raining or snowing. Compact cameras in which the flash and the lens are close together are particularly susceptible to this problem.

Fuji, many feel, could have done a better job of presenting the case. To begin with, their opening paragraph makes it sound as though every image produced with a flash is going to contain round, white spots, and that is far from the truth.

Indeed, the beam of a motion picture projector will clearly show circulating dust particles, but the average person can more easily observe them in any home where a beam of sunlight has penetrated a gloomy room.

There is no such thing as a dust-free environment, indoors or out. Minute particles are everywhere, and the more activity that occurs in an area, the more they are stirred up. But it is not simply a matter of light reflecting from dust particles; it takes a certain set of circumstances.

Flash units in compact digital cameras are built into the body of the unit and very close to the lens, while in older cameras they were usually elevated or off to one side and frequently on a different plane than the lens. When the light source is placed close to the lens and on the same level, the area immediately in front of the lens is brilliantly illuminated when the picture is snapped.

Although a particle suspended in the air is usually very tiny, its close proximity to the lens will make it appear much larger. And because it is so close, it will also be out of focus and normally appear as a sphere.

All kinds of particles in the atmosphere can produce an orb or sometimes a fairy-like image in a photograph. In addition to dust, examples include pollen grains, aerosol particles, rain, snow and other moisture as well as insects. And human activity, wind, humidity, temperature and other geographical conditions can dictate the concentration of such material.

Because of the brief duration of a flash and because the photographer is looking through the viewfinder at a more distant subject, he or she does not notice these particles at the time of exposure. The operation of many cameras also blocks one's view at the precise second the photo is being taken.

Other arguments can be made about the fact that most inexpensive cameras utilize fixed-focus lenses and that digital imaging is markedly different from traditional film photography and often far inferior in detail, but the factors above, which can easily be tested by anyone, explain nearly every "ghost orb" photograph I have seen.

The conclusion to an objective observer seems clear—that at least the large majority of orb images in photographs are caused by reflection of light from tiny objects close to the camera lens and are not intelligent entities from some hidden level of reality.

Many people want to believe in the supernatural. Rare are those who pursue evidence wherever it leads and accept it regardless of how the results match up with their hopes and egos, but the tide of recklessness seems to be turning. Not all ghost hunters and ghost societies blindly accept digital photographs of orbs as evidence of the supernatural. "There are ghost hunters and ghost wanters," a member of the Pennsylvania Ghost Hunters Society explains. "The wanters see a ghost in everything."

"Dust is the most common anomaly that will be photographed by the beginning ghost hunter," states a posting by the International Ghost Hunters Society. "Ghost research is more than just snapping a few digital photos that capture an orb or multiple orbs and thinking that these orbs might be spirits. One of the best things that a new ghost hunter could do is take a hundred photos of dust, pollen, rain droplets or other anomalies found in their location to establish a base line to compare later photos. A base line is important because a location might have unique anomalies. For example, in Yuma, Arizona, the anomalies are a fine sand that is suspended in the air when the wind blows and will appear different than dust or pollen. Unfortunately, orbs captured with a lower resolution camera may not provide sufficient resolution between natural anomalies and spirit anomalies for analysis. Suspect photos should be compared to previous orbs captured with the same camera. It is so important to pay attention to the small details about the orbs. Do not assume that every bright orb is a spirit orb. Bright orbs may be resulting because the anomaly was too close to the lens when the flash discharged."

Another group, the Toronto and Ontario Ghosts and Hauntings Research Society, no longer accepts orb photographs unless they meet very strict environmental controls and physical descriptions. "We are still looking for a particular type of orb photo," a representative is quoted as saying, "and so far, no luck."

Dr. Ken, co-founder of the Ohio Ghost Hunters Society, has posted a lot of sound information on orbs, which he calls the most common form of spirit photography. "Don't take everything odd looking in a photo as a ghost," Dr. Ken warns and goes on to discuss "ghosts" that result from camera or developing glitches, lens flare, lens flash, hair, breath, dust on the lens, over and under exposed film, old film, film that's been overheated etc.

And what does Dr. Ken have to say about digital cameras? "Stay away from them for ghost hunting. They do not work! Any dust in the air will be amplified 1,000 times and show up much brighter than usual. A lot of digital photos will produce multiple orbs. This is either due to low light or lots of dust."

A spokesman for the Umbria Paranormal Research Team reports, "We do not use digital cameras and refuse to allow those who investigate with us to use them. We spent some time e-mailing around to several manufacturers of digital cameras as well as several professional photographers, and each provided a plausible mechanical explanation for the presence of orbs on a photograph taken with a digital camera. Bottom line: We do not trust the 'science' or the 'evidence' that digital photography produces, and we do not support, advocate, or even believe in the use of such cameras in the field of paranormal research."

It is the philosophy of the American Ghost Society to attempt to rule out every natural explanation for a potential haunting before considering the idea that the cause of the phenomena might be a ghost. Troy Taylor, AGS founder and president, believes that the misuse of digital cameras by the general public has led to a disastrous loss of credibility for all paranormal investigators and is making a mockery of spirit photography. After photographing orbs with digital cameras and consulting with engineers and technical support staff at major camera manufacturers, Taylor has concluded that the cameras create the orbs.

Finally, we have the view of the general scientific community, and it should come as no surprise that it fails to support a supernatural explanation for orb photographs.

The Committee for the Scientific Investigation of Claims of the

Paranormal, CSICOP, is an international network of scientists, researchers and academics devoted to the scientific investigation and evaluation of claims of the paranormal and pseudoscience. The last time I checked, its roster included five Nobel laureates as well as numerous other respected scholars. CSICOP publishes the highly acclaimed *Skeptical Inquirer*, the magazine for science and reason.

Dr. Robert Baker, professor emeritus in psychology at the University of Kentucky, a CSICOP fellow and member of the Association for Rational Thought, says there are scientific reasons for all mysterious sounds, sights and instrument readings. Though he is intrigued by ghost stories, he has never found evidence of the paranormal.

Baker is convinced that man's belief in ghosts is the result of his strong desire to believe in life after death and, therefore, to expect events that demonstrate such a belief. "There are no such things as haunted houses," Dr. Baker contends. "There are only haunted people."

Boaz Bell's Gravestone

With a Pot
on His Head

"**G**o to the end of the fence," Richard Jamieson had directed, "and take the road to the left."

The byway that parallels the barrier is a narrow and slightly sunken dirt lane, and it offered an ample scattering of mud holes to dodge on the day I traveled there in search of Boaz Bell's grave.

Where the enclosure makes a right-angle turn to the left, I obeyed Jamieson's instructions and proceeded down an even more confining artery that led through a forest of mixed hardwood and pine. Small metal signs nailed to trees at intervals informed me that I had entered Delaware Gamelands.

After another mile, I had been told, I would encounter a roadblock constructed of tree trunks piled with dirt, but a deep, wide, water-filled depression interrupted my progress after no more than several hundred yards. I knew before stepping out to investigate that any attempt to navigate the wallow in my Voyager would pose too great a risk. I locked the van, slipped my cell phone into a back pocket, slung a camera over my shoulder and advanced down the lane on foot.

"Make a right at the logs and mound of dirt," Jamieson's instructions had continued, "and walk about half a mile to a stream that goes under the road. Then back up fifty yards and go straight into the woods towards Broad Creek."

When I reached the pile of dirt and logs and stepped around them, I began to seriously question my guide's idea of what constitutes a road. After leaving the hard surface of Delaware 78, each turn had presented a less appealing thoroughfare. The pathway I now faced may have carried wagons or lumber carts at one time, but it was little more than a trail now, kept open by the boots of hunters. A felled pine placed precisely to block its entrance seemed unnecessary; I would certainly never attempt to drive beyond that point.

As I progressed through the damp woods, I occasionally caught a glimpse of Broad Creek, winding around fringes of marsh and woods from the town of Laurel to its collision with the Nanticoke River, less than a mile distant. A cool sun sparkled on the water's lightly ruffled surface, which shone through the tangle of trees and vines like a rippling ribbon of molten silver. With no visible sign of humankind to break the spell, I walked in another time, trying to imagine what it must have been like to live on those sandy dunes at the onset of the nineteenth century, when the only sound of commerce was the creak of oars and the snap of canvas sails in the wind.

It was early winter, and a thick carpet of recently fallen leaves disguised many small features on the surface of the land. Had I been even slightly distracted as I passed it, I would have missed the trickle of water that crossed through a narrow concrete pipe beneath the trail. I turned, backtracked fifty paces and headed at right angles into the woods in the direction of Broad Creek.

Dick Jamieson and I might enjoy debating the difference between roads and trails and streams and springs someday, but he knows how to give directions. After picking my way through brush and greenbrier for no more than seventy-five yards, I walked directly into what remains of a wrought iron fence around the graveyard; and the first two stones I encountered each bore the carved name of Boaz Bell—father and son.

Delaware Records: Sussex County Tombstones, a report posted on the Internet and dated January 1967, describes the location of this graveyard as "near Ward's Corner and Pepperbox Road, Little Creek Hundred, Sussex County." Like so many things floating around in Cyberspace, the information is incorrect. If I had gone to Pepperbox Road at Ward's Corner, I would have been more than twelve miles off course as the crow flies—a lot more via several Delaware highways.

Other Bells also lie at rest here: Mary; three children who barely made it past their first birthdays; and Lavinia, who died at the age of seventeen. And there are monuments to Asbury and Mary Insley; to Eglantine and Genevieve Adams (such elegant names); to Edward Barton and to Sarah Cannon, "Consort of Isaac Cannon."

The grave of Sarah, which has been heavily vandalized, presents one of several mysteries. In the Bell family Bible it is recorded that *Mary* Bell married Isaac Cannon on the 26th day of April in 1803, and that her sister *Sarah* died on the 22nd day of October 1775, having lived but eleven days.

And to the right of the elder Boaz's grave lies *Mary*, "Consort of Boaz;" yet the Bible informs us that Boaz married *Mager* Twyford on the 20th day of November in 1799, and Dorchester County records confirm the union and the date. (This section of Sussex County was once part of Maryland and then of Pennsylvania before it became Delaware.) Does Mager equal Mary? No one I have consulted believes that to be so.

I spread shaving cream on a small square of cardboard and gently rubbed it across the elder Boaz's inscription, filling the depressions to make them easier to read:

In memory of
BOAZ BELL
Who departed this life
January 11th, 1837
Aged 65 years 8 months
And 9 days.

The Internet posting cited above records the year of Boaz's death as 1857, and the stone appears to confirm that at first glance. But the family Bible lists his date of birth as "Thursday 2nd May 1771." Do the math and the year comes out to 1837, not 1857. The numerals 3 and 5 are often confused on old, worn monuments.

And what was it that had aroused my interest in Captain Boaz Bell (all of the early Bells were men of the sea)? Oral tradition and a brief comment in several books of Delaware history claim that Boaz Bell was known for walking across the Nanticoke River bottom with a "bell" or a "pot" on his head. One area resident added that he could be heard laughing during his traverse, and none of the sources had anything further to offer.

I wanted more.

Everett Conaway and John Knowles are cousins and descendants of Nathaniel Bell and Sarah Jauncey Bell, who were natives of Bermuda and the parents of Boaz. Conaway, an octogenarian, lives on Belfast, the original estate acquired by Nathaniel and Sarah in the latter half of the eighteenth century, a property that once extended from the Nanticoke to the town of Bethel and contained more than two thousand acres.

As the three of us examined family documents and photographs in the living room of the current Belfast home, Conaway said, "The Bells were traders. They went back and forth all the time between the Nanticoke and Bermuda."

The family Bible indicates that some of Nathaniel and Sarah's children were born on the British owned island and others at Belfast in Delaware. Their three-century-old Bermuda homestead remains standing and is occupied to the present day.

I mentioned to Conaway that the length of Boaz's grave had immediately impressed me. The measurements of nearly every vault I have ever taped, as well as distances between headstones and footstones of in-ground burials, clearly demonstrate that most of our early settlers were short of stature, averaging little more than five feet in height. My hiking boots measure exactly twelve inches in length, and I laid them down seven times between the headstones and footstones of both Boaz Bell graves. Others in the yard conform to expected dimensions.

"He was said to stand six foot four in his stocking feet—the one that carried the pot across the river," Belfast's current resident replied. "He carried a hog pot—a big hog pot. Put it over his head for air and walked across the river. I got that from my grandfather."

"And which Boaz was it that made the walk?"

"The one that had two wives. And they both sailed on the boat with him. He must have been a Mormon or something. I don't know how many children he had."

"And why did he walk across the river?" I wanted to know.

"He made a bet," came the quick reply. "He bet one of his wives for a carriage and horses. I don't know which one. I think that's recorded up in Dover, but I'm not sure. He bet the man that owned the carriage. He bet the wife against the carriage and horses."

"And where did this happen?"

"Boaz owned Cherry Walk, which was right below Belfast on the river. I always thought he walked across here, somewhere."

Old kettles and pots were generally made of iron and came in various sizes. They were used to cook everything from soup to soap, even for blanching hogs to remove their hair before butchering. Early experiments that eventually led to our modern diving bells were conducted with just such devices. They trapped air when inverted and were placed over the diver's head as he entered the water.

Aristotle observed and reported such practices as early as the fourth century BC: "They enable the divers to respire equally well by letting down a cauldron," he wrote, "for this does not fill with water, but retains the air, for it is forced straight down into the water."

While the weight of such a device is cumbersome on land, the trapped air will displace much of the burden when submerged. Besides, a body needs to be weighted down in order for it to be able to gain a foot purchase on the bottom. Modern divers use lead belts to keep them submerged.

Neither Conaway nor Knowles could provide any specific information on Boaz's alleged two wives. The Bible and county records say he married Mager; yet Mary lies in the grave beside him. If he married both, where are the records for Mary and where does Mager rest?

One census report indicates that the younger Boaz was married to "Mary J.," but this cannot be the Mary buried next to the elder Boaz. She was twenty-one when the younger Boaz was born and would appear to be his mother. Two Mary Bells are listed on a later census of the area, but we have no way of knowing whether they were widowed or never married.

Then Conaway surprised me with another story I had never heard before. "Patty Cannon stole some slaves from Boaz and killed them all up on that hill. There were four of them, Pop used to say. They used to call it Patty Cannon's Hill. They were very superstitious, and nobody wanted to go over that hill at night. Of course they all had slaves. There were eight slave huts here at one time. Boaz told her if he ever caught her on this side of the river again, he'd kill her. They said he picked her right up."

Is it likely that Boaz Bell had such an encounter with the infamous Patty Cannon? The first question that arises is why she would have killed four slaves that she had just kidnapped. She was, after all, in the slave trading business, and four captives might have been sold on the southern market for as much as three to four thousand dollars, a lot of money in those days.

Another bit of historical trivia also raises a question about whether there was animosity between the Bells and Cannons. Joe Johnson, Patty's son-in-law, was arrested at the Cannon residence in 1821 on kidnapping charges. The evidence against him included testimony that one of the victims had been kidnapped in Baltimore and brought from there to the Nanticoke River on a vessel commanded by Captain William Bell, who was Boaz's brother. Delaware officials indicted William on a number of kidnapping charges, all of which were eventually dismissed when authorities failed to apprehend him.

At the edge of Belfast, where the road rises slightly as it comes from Woodland Ferry, an incident occurred in 1811 or 1812 that may be at the root of Conaway's story. Henry Brereton, in company with John and Jesse Griffith, intercepted two slave traders with the intent of robbing them. The victims escaped to Laurel, though one was mortally wounded in the ambush. After Jesse Griffith turned state's evidence against his brother and Brereton, the pair was hanged. Unsupported tradition claims that Patty—dressed in a man's clothing and carrying a musket—led the attack on the traders' carriage.

Several of my friends have suggested that on a peninsula so rich in culture and history, surely there is room for one more celebration. How about a Boaz Bell River Walk Festival?

Bring your own hog pot.

Everett Conaway and Jack Knowles Examine Bell Land Records

What I Did
This Summer

When children across the nation return to school each September, one of the first assignments many of them have to face is an essay titled "What I Did This Summer."

As a teen, I avidly read the Little Abner comic strip, never realizing at the time that cartoonist Al Capp's contributions to American culture would far transcend the cartoon page. He gave us words and expressions like druthers and irregardless; Kickapoo Joy Juice, that colossally potent beverage; and Lower Slobbovia, the most miserable place to live on earth. And who among our senior citizens can forget the birth of the Shmoo in 1948, that lovable glob with the bewhiskered smile and button eyes that took the nation by storm.

The Shmoo consumed essentially nothing, bred with a speed that put rabbits to shame and provided nearly every staple necessary to sustain humankind. Besides producing an endless supply of milk and eggs, its meat was pork when roasted, chicken when fried and steak when broiled—and the little varmint took sheer delight in being eaten.

The heyday of the Shmoo inspired one of our first licensed-product bonanzas, and a cornucopia of items spawned nearly as fast as the Shmoos themselves. As I was writing this, I made a quick search of the eBay auction site and discovered a variety of Shmoo collectibles: books, statues, plates, glasses, hand fans, jewelry, a key chain puzzle, pin-backs, shakers, banks, play money, a room deodorizer holder and a pilot show film among them.

Every now and then a scraggier than usual character made his appearance in Dogpatch. His last name was an unpronounceable collection of consonants, and a black cloud followed Joe Btfsplk wherever he went, continuously soaking him with rain. He was feared and shunned by all. He was the world's worst jinx.

In my "golden years" I have come to appreciate a little of how poor Joe must have felt, going through life as a paragon of misfortune. Those who have read my story "Thank You for Calling Horizon" will have a small grasp of what I mean. My numerous misadventures with the mega telephone service provider Veriz... (Whoops) Horizon are but a small chapter in the still expanding epic of the curse that pursues me through life. But I started to tell you about what I did this summer. What I did this summer was take a three-month computer journey from Point A to Point A.

I understand (oh, how I understand) that the mere mention of the word "computer" brings many of my fellow seniors to fits of trembling and mumbling, but I shall lead slowly with this tale and provide what I hope will be adequate technical assistance as we go along.

Load: (verb) to place something on or aboard. In this story we will use the term when referring to the process of loading software onto hardware. Hmm, I guess that calls for additional definitions.

Hardware: (noun) the stuff made of metal and plastic and silicon that sits on your desk—the computer, the keyboard, the printer, the scanner....

Software: (noun) the stuff you can't see that makes the hardware do things. Software comes on compact disks today, like music. You put the disk into a slot on the computer and an icon appears on your desktop.

Icon: (noun) a small picture or symbol that represents something else.

Desktop: (noun) what you see on your display when you boot up the computer.

Display: (noun) the screen that lights up when you turn your computer on. Think TV.

Boot up: (verb) to turn your computer on.

Now, where was I? Oh, yes, we were explaining how one loads software onto hardware. When you put the disk containing the software into the slot on the computer, an icon pops up on your display and....

I can see this isn't going to work. I simply won't have enough space to explain it all. If I say something you don't understand, you will just have to ask your (or somebody's) granddaughter to explain it to you. Every six-year-old in America knows more about computers than you or I ever will.

My first Apple computer lost its hard drive two years ago and was replaced by a newer and better model (and the day after *any* computer is delivered to you, there is always a newer and better model available). For a while I was thrilled with my Power Mac; then, beginning with small aberrations at first, its performance became quite erratic. By the spring of this year, my hardware was giving me a bloody fit, blinking and freezing and destroying copy every few seconds. I called Apple technical support.

The technician was cheery and courteous. He assisted me in renewing my operating system. I reloaded my word and photo processing software and reinstalled my printer and scanner, and for a while things returned to normal—a very short while. The blinking and freezing returned and I called Apple again.

As the weeks progressed, the sequence became a ritual. I was considering ways to establish an open line to Apple or, perhaps, offer my guestroom as a permanent residence to one of their technicians. Eventually, on something like the 132nd call (well, that may be a slight exaggeration), Apple instructed me to take the computer to an authorized service center and have them check the processor and logic board.

To the owner of a service center, the words "check" and "replace" are synonymous, and then he looks for something else he might be able to add to the toll. In my case the something else was a new hard drive (your granddaughter will quickly let you know that the hard drive is the heart of a computer and a very pricey item).

Since I was the proud owner of an Apple Protection Plan, Apple paid the bill. I had a practically new computer and it hadn't cost me a penny—just weeks of stress. My world was about to take a huge turn for the better.

As your granddaughter would put it: "Not!"

Within a week, the Power Mac was back to blinking and freezing. I decided that I could not continue to live with the problem. Something had to give, and one learns early on when dealing with computers that the something is always *you*. Time for Plan B—or was it Z by now? I decided to buy a second computer.

My new Mac came with the latest operating system (although an update was recommended by Apple a week afterward), and I also purchased the most recent Microsoft Office and Adobe PhotoShop software. Loaded together, they purred like a bed full of happy kittens. There was only one problem: So much had been redesigned since my old computer had been manufactured (two years ago), that my $1000 laser printer and $300 scanner could not be connected to the new computer. What now?

The old Mac had a new hard drive, processor, etc., and I had become convinced that my problems with it lay in a conflict between software programs. I was the proud owner of a new operating system and the latest software necessary to continue my work. Lights flashed. Bells chimed. I would strip the hard drive, load the new software and have two perfectly purring machines as well as the use of my scanner and laser printer. All would be right in the world again.

Not!

The printer and scanner software refused to load with the new programs. It was compatible only with the old operating system, a message on my display explained to me.

I called Apple, discussed what I had done and the dilemma I now faced. The technician carried me through several checks and eventually instructed me to go the Hewlett Packard website and download the latest software for my scanner and printer, which would update them to the new Apple operating system. HP is the manufacturer of my printer and scanner.

The downloads, which consumed quite a bit of time, helped not a bit, and additional calls were required to determine that Hewlett Packard had not yet posted the programs necessary to resolve my predicament; but an Apple technician gave me a phone number at HP, where, he assured me, I was certain to find a live person to provide assistance.

The people at Hewlett Packard are extremely courteous. The woman who answered listened to my tale of woe and put me in touch with a technician whose specialty was the LaserJet 2100 series. And she had other good news: "We're down at the moment," she said, "so I won't charge you for the call."

The printer specialist agreed that HP was not up-to-date with their software postings, but he could carry me through a procedure to solve my problem—and he did. After half an hour of guided adjustments, my LaserJet whirred to life and kicked out a beautifully printed document.

"Now, what about my scanner?" I asked.

He transferred me to a ScanJet specialist, a delightful conversationalist who also managed to get the scanner working again. There was a glitch, however: The scanner software only worked with Apple's old operating system.

"No problem at all," the charming lady advised me. "Your new operating system contains the necessary elements of the old system to make your scanner function. All you have to do is choose the old system when you want to use it," and she led me through the procedure.

"And how do I get back into the new system?"

"Just reverse the process."

I reached through the telephone and gave her a huge hug, thanked her profusely and offered to wash her windows and do her laundry for the rest of my life; then I took a break and made dinner.

After the dishes were washed, I fired up the computer again, but nothing I could do would get me into the new operating system—it had vanished!

"It's there," an out-of-state friend responded to my telephone plea for help (the professional techs had all quit for the day and gone home to their wives); "we just have to figure out how to get to it." He would work on the problem and get back to me in the morning.

The next morning dawned. We talked. We failed.

I called Apple again, provided a long review of the problem and was instructed to go to their website and download a series of updates.

Nine hours and twenty minutes later, I called it a day and sent a progress report to a few of my friends.

"God Love you!" one responded.

"She gave up on me a long time ago," I replied.

On the following morning I arose bright and cheery, hopeful of a solution before the sun would set again. After completing the final downloads—another seven hours—I excitedly began the process of installing the collection of items on my hard drive. A window immediately popped up informing me that it wasn't going to happen.

I called Apple, offered my case number to the answering technician and told him that my hard drive refused to accept the two days worth of downloads. He clearly did not know what I was talking about.

I recited the titles of the updates that had been downloaded.

He did not understand why they had taken so long.

I explained that I had simply followed the last technician's directions to download each unit of the programs separately, a total of twenty-one parts in all.

He contemptuously muttered that there was no such notation on the case record. The only entry had been made a week earlier by the first of five technicians, who indicated that he had assisted me in the process of "configuring my computer."

I began to outline the weeklong struggle to ford my latest quagmire, but the young gentleman with the burr in his trousers interrupted after a few sentences and bluntly informed me that he could not provide further support as I was in violation of the Apple software agreement.

The word "astonishment" does not come close to covering the impact of his words, but I quickly regained my composure and patiently reminded him that five other Apple technicians had worked with me during the past seven days.

He didn't care how many others had taken on my problem; he wasn't going to.

I begged for an explanation.

In a voice that spewed venom, he informed me that I might have purchased two computers from Apple, but the program I had acquired with one of them could not, by policy, be used with the other. If I wanted to load their new operating system on my older computer, I would have to purchase a second copy for another $120.

I remained surprisingly calm and told him I wished to speak to his supervisor.

After an eight-minute wait, a new voice apologized for the delay and offered to listen to my concerns.

I reviewed The Week (I shall forever think of it as written with capital letters), and the gentleman began to patiently lead me through procedures to load the updates.

We moved items in and out of folders, off and onto the hard drive, in and out of the trash. We rearranged everything—then we rearranged the rearrangements. We mixed and matched. But in spite of all our efforts, the updates refused to load.

After nearly an hour of failure, I, who doesn't have a clue about the internal workings of a computer (and doesn't want to), wondered out loud if it might not be best to strip the hard drive and begin from step one.

"You may be right," the Apple voice replied.

We did that and things began to load. Since the whole process was going to take a while and I understood the steps to take, I thanked the gentleman for his assistance and bid him farewell.

Each of the programs and updates loaded in turn, and when I finally completed the task, the computer was functioning like a finely tuned clock—and the printer and scanner lay uselessly dead beside it. I was squarely back to where I had been seven days earlier.

I did not sleep well that night and had business on the road the next day in another part of the state. When I returned, I sent an e-mail to update my friends.

"I can understand why you failed to put a subject on your e-mail," replied one. "There is none that covers it. The only conclusion I can reach is that somewhere along the way you screwed the computer gods without knowing it. Why not try taking your computer to bed with you and holding it close and asking for forgiveness."

"Remember," another offered, "it was an apple that started the mess in the Garden of Eden!"

My son wrote: "You should have bought a Dell, dude."

Back when I purchased my first computer and a technician was helping me to struggle through some now-forgotten problem, he made the casual remark: "Some people weren't meant to own a computer."

Surely, he couldn't have been talking about *me*?

Postscript: Since this article was written, all computer companies have begun to outsource their telephone technical services to the Asian subcontinent. You think things used to be tough?

Living in a Vortex

My unabridged edition of the *Random House Dictionary of the English Language* provides a variety of definitions for "vortex," some of them a bit confusing to the non-scientific mind. But we can all picture whirling masses of air or water, such as tornados and whirlpools—forces that draw into their powerful currents everything that crosses their paths. A vortex may even be composed of flame. Consider Elijah, who, it is written, was taken away in a "fiery whirlwind."

Fans of the paranormal often speak of invisible funnels or vortices into which people and other things disappear—objects sometimes as large as an ocean liner. Who hasn't heard stories of the Bermuda Triangle, also referred to as Devil's Triangle, Hoodoo Sea or Limbo of the Lost—a region of the Atlantic Ocean between Bermuda, Fort Lauderdale, Florida, and San Juan, Puerto Rico, into which some seventy-five aircraft and perhaps more than 2,000 ships have gone missing over the years?

Some claim that Christopher Columbus was the first European to bear witness to the perils of the Bermuda Triangle. As the *Nina, Pinta* and *Santa Maria* sailed through the area in 1492, Columbus recorded unusual compass readings, and he and his crew saw strange lights in the sky. His journal mentions "a great flame of fire" that crashed into the ocean, most likely a meteor.

The Triangle legend gained momentum after December 5, 1945, when five U. S. Navy Avenger bombers vanished while on a routine training mission from Ft. Lauderdale, followed by the Martin Mariner rescue plane that was sent to search for them. When you examine the facts relating to the loss of Flight 19, it is less mysterious than some would make it out to be, but you will have to research that for yourselves; I'm getting too far off the course of the story I want to tell.

Disappearances tend to fascinate and stir the imagination. One popular theory outside the scientific community is that the Bermuda Triangle contains a vortex into which objects are drawn and held in a different interval or space—a time warp, if you will.

As cynical as one might be about the existence of parallel time differentials, scientists, if I understand correctly, do believe that all matter exists in a whirling, spiral motion. Whether we are talking about a galaxy, a sun, a planet or something as small as an atom, all things, I have read, rotate on an axis and revolve around a core. This natural action of energy is called "vortex kinesis."

But if I am to accept such a notion, it can only be as an act of faith. Both space (infinite largeness) and atoms (infinite smallness) are things that truly boggle my mind. I never would have come to understand that I actually *live* in a vortex if it hadn't been for the old man. The old man knew how to explain such esoteric principles in simple, down-to-earth English.

When I purchased my twenty-six acres at public auction in 1972, most who lived in the general vicinity referred to the property as "back there." It was, indeed, *back there*—situated on a single-lane dirt artery that generated a swirling, choking cloud of dust whenever a vehicle strayed my way in dry weather. But during a spring thaw or after several rainy days, the branch quickly evolved into a muddy, car-and-tractor-swallowing morass. From my front doorstep, the ribbon of earth meandered a mile through woods to a paved county road in one direction—half a mile in the other. I loved being *back there* then and still do, though in the ensuing years I have gained a near and good neighbor, and the county has improved access by laying one lane of asphalt on the half-mile end of the still-less-traveled byway.

As the first autumn of my happy proprietorship settled in, I reveled in the brisk mornings, the abundant wildlife, the bright orange and yellow and the sporty crimson hues of the season's foliage, but I soon noticed something unusual about the frost. Often, though it lay heavy and hoary on my roof and yard, there was none in sight by the time I reached the state road.

One morning I mentioned this phenomenon to an old man who lived nearby and had befriended me. "What you got *back there*," he quickly explained, "is a frost pocket. Your place just sucks that frost right down and holds it there."

O.K., so I was the proud caretaker of a "frost pocket." I figured I could live with that. There are a lot of worse things in this world than a place that sucks the frost down.

If you allow woods to grow and mature naturally on the Eastern Shore of Maryland, they tend to be dense and harbor a multitude of flying, crawling, stinging, biting and sucking creatures when the weather is warm, a few of which can cause not only discomfort but genuine bodily harm. Lyme disease and West Nile virus are only two in the news these days. I prefer winter woods for hiking and investigating nature, and I spent a lot of time in mine that first cold season.

During my lifetime I have sauntered uncounted miles across many fields and through a multitude of forests. I have trudged canyons and deserts, climbed mountains and run rivers in boats and canoes, and I vaguely recall finding a spent balloon once or twice. I am speaking, of course, of the toy variety that you fill with air from your lungs or with helium from a tank and often tie to a ribbon or string. I was totally unprepared for what was lurking on my tiny piece of Delmarva. I wish now that I had kept them all or at least made a record. I have no idea how many balloons I have found on my acres over the years, but there have been a lot of them.

I believe I came across three in as many woodland sojourns that first fall, two of the small, common rubber variety and one of the larger plastic breed. All had strings attached, and the latter bore the message: "Happy Birthday!"

I recall one after that with a smiling Mickey Mouse, another with a message that escapes me now, and I once came across a plastic inflatable dangling a festive array of multicolored ribbons and imprinted with the grinning image of Garfield, that fat, lazy, sarcastic, bedeviling, lasagna-eating cat of cartoon fame. The balloon hadn't completely deflated nor quite reached the ground, having been snared by its ribbons on an alder shrub.

I believe it was during the second or third year that I mentioned the balloons to a friend, who simply shrugged. Shortly after that I picked up the remains of a bright red, rubber variety that had burst but still held a message from an elementary school student in Montgomery County, Maryland. Children there had sponsored a balloon release, and the note requested a reply so they could determine which missile had traveled the farthest. I showed it to the old man and for the first time told him about all the others I had found.

"What you got *back there*," my white-haired sage responded without a moment's hesitation and with an authority honed by years of accumulated knowledge and experience, "is a place that sucks them balloons right down. There's places that attracts things like that, and that's just what you got *back there*."

But of course! How could I not have understood?

Since then I have discovered others, including a second from a mass release on the Western shores of Chesapeake Bay. From its appearance, it had been in the woods for some time, but the address was still readable and I replied.

Physical limitations in recent years have prevented me from spending as much time as I would like in the woods, but I'm sure those balloons are out there, still being sucked down out of the sky by my own little vortex. If any wayward balloons are listening, beware as you approach District 3 in Dorchester County.

During my first winter on the Shore, I gave no special thought to several large, dead trees in various stages of decay that I found scattered throughout the woods. Trees die for a variety of reasons and all forests contain such remains, but I came across one large loblolly pine that had obviously succumbed to a lightning strike.

The long, spiral split in its bark was no more than a few months old.

Lightning strikes to trees are common, and I have seen them wherever tall sentinels rise toward thunderheads. Sometimes the victim survives, but the tremendous heat displaced by the bolt more often explodes sap-filled veins that carry nourishment from earth to crown, and the slow process of rot begins.

Delmarva has its share of torrid summer storms, and at least two more trees on my property were hit in the ensuing summer—a large pine in the west woods and a sweet gum near the boundary to the east. The pine displayed a telltale, spiral split in the bark, while the gum had been splintered thirty feet above the forest floor, sending its crown crashing down and burying the upper trunk two feet in the moist earth. Electrocution claimed at least two additional pines during the third and fourth summers.

It was about 1977 that I began growing tomatoes on a trellis in a small garden next to the old tenant house. I set four oak posts eight feet apart and strung three, heavy-gauge wires from post to post at two-foot internals from the ground, securing them with heavy staples to the posts. As the pruned tomato plants grew upward, I tied them to the wires. By mid summer, the trellis was producing more fruit than my friends and I could consume.

Then, after an absence of several days in August, I returned to find the first and third poles split and splayed for nearly their entire length, and every tomato plant hung brown and wilted from the wires. Clearly, the supports had been struck by lightning and the wires had conducted the current through the entire trellis, zapping every plant in the process.

As word of the tomato disaster spread from the bench of a nearby country store, my garden quickly became a community tourist destination. It was then that I mentioned to the old man for the first time what I considered to be an uncommon number of electrical hits to my property.

"You got one of them places *back there* that attracts lightnin'," he replied with his usual air of authority. "There's places like that. It's an old fool's yarn that lightnin' never strikes the same place mor'n once. It hits some over and over again, and that's just what you got *back there.* Your place just sucks that lightnin' right down."

Predictably, the heavenly fire has continued to be sucked down *back there.* The west woods has lost several more giants, and the thick bed of dry humus beneath a struck pine was once set on fire and smoldered for several days before being discovered.

A bluebird nesting box, which I had mounted on a six-foot post only fifty feet from my front porch, literally exploded when the picket was split in a blinding, ear-shattering strike during a summer afternoon storm. I found splinters of cedar wood scattered as far as ninety feet in one direction and eighty-two in another. Fortunately, the box was unoccupied at the time.

Thirty-three pines that I planted as seedlings between the house and road stand more than fifty feet tall, and the largest is eighty inches in circumference. There *were* thirty-six loblollies in the twin rows at one time, but three have rotted to barely discernable stumps, having been killed over the years by lightning. Three others were split by a single strike eight years ago and survived.

When I returned home after dark one evening last September from a library program, my neighbor called to say there had been a horrendous crash during a thunderstorm in my absence, and a brief ball of flame had been seen among the pines between our houses. Daylight revealed broad, spiraling gashes in the bark of two of the pines that had endured the earlier strike. It was immediately clear that they weren't going to make it this time.

And so it is, as I explained earlier, that I live in a vortex. I still love it *back there,* but I keep hoping to find some way to get the old homestead to suck down a little money now and then.

Postscript: During the evening of the day I finished writing this account, I was talking on the telephone to a friend in Pennsylvania and mentioned the distant rumble of an approaching storm. Before we were able to terminate our conversation, my receiver crackled loudly to the accompaniment of a bright flash and a tremendous clap of thunder. Neither the phone nor I were injured, but another beloved pine had fallen victim to the Maiden Branch Vortex.

Above: President Warfield at Her Norfolk Pier in 1939

Below: U.S.S President Warfield (IX-169) at Norfolk in 1945

A Tale of Two Ships

B etween the 1813 launching of *Chesapeake*, a 130-foot wooden craft designed along the lines of a schooner, and the 1963 retirement of *Bay Belle*, an all steel, 300-foot, four-decked packet, more than 600 steamboats plied the waters of Chesapeake Bay and threaded their way through 2,000 miles of the estuary's navigable rivers, connecting merchants and planters in isolated communities to the markets of Baltimore and Norfolk and the general public to the region's special services and cultural attractions.

No one can dispute the impact that steamers had on the development of Tidewater Maryland and Virginia, but the smoke-belching vessels provided more than transportation, they became the heart and soul of a romantic era that has never been equaled on the Chesapeake. Steamboatin' days are remembered as a time when life was good and progress advanced at a more measured, leisurely pace.

The Baltimore Steam Packet Company, more commonly known as the Old Bay Line, began its service in 1839 under an act of the Maryland General Assembly. Two of its founding officials had connections to the original bay steamer, *Chesapeake*. Through good and bad times, the line generally prospered during the nineteenth century, gaining fame especially for the meals it served.

Shortly after the turn of the twentieth century, Seaboard Air Line Railroad purchased Old Bay's entire capital stock. The two corporations, however, continued to operate independently. World War I more than doubled shipping and transportation demand, yet when the government took over management of railroad and steamboat lines as a war measure in 1918, neglect and depreciation swiftly followed.

Solomon Davies Warfield was elected to head the Old Bay Line in 1918 but was unable to exercise his office until the government returned transportation lines to their owners in 1920. Once at his desk, the new president moved to invigorate the company by constructing a series of faster and more luxurious, steel-hulled packets. The first keel was laid on March 4, 1922, and the *State of Maryland* sailed on her maiden voyage from Baltimore to Norfolk on January 6, 1923.

The *State of Virginia* followed, and Warfield ordered a third vessel in 1927—tentatively named *Florida*—to be constructed at the Pusey and Jones shipyard on the Christiana River in Wilmington, Delaware, but before *Florida* could be completed, the Old Bay executive died. When she was eventually launched, company officials christened her *President Warfield* in memory of the man who had set the line back on its feet.

The *Warfield* made her proud debut on Chesapeake Bay on Friday, July 13, 1928. There she would spend most of the next fourteen years as the proclaimed queen of the estuary, cruising leisurely on overnight runs between Baltimore and Norfolk and for a brief while as a charter boat between New York and Boston.

A palatial, three-decked vessel measuring 330 feet in length and fifty-eight in the beam, the *President Warfield* boasted elaborately paneled saloons, smoking rooms designed to look like British pubs, glass-enclosed palm rooms on her gallery deck, and grand stairways and balconies hung with chandeliers and oil paintings. She boasted 170 first-class staterooms, thirty-eight with private baths. In spite of the Great Depression and the fact that steamboats were rapidly declining as a primary choice of transportation, the grand lady with a man's name remained popular with many who wanted to hold on to an old and beloved maritime tradition or who simply enjoyed the boat's elegant amenities and stress-free pace of travel.

Then came World War II, and on June 11, 1942, a decree from the U. S. War Shipping Administration ended the luxury steamer's quiet life on the Chesapeake. Much of the *Warfield's* interior fittings and passenger accommodations were removed in a Baltimore ship-yard, and foredecks and openings were covered with turtle-back shields and planking against the boarding seas she would encounter on the North Atlantic. Her superstructure was cut back nearly to the funnel to add a navigation bridge and pilothouse. Freighter masts and cargo booms were installed along with tubs mounting twenty-millimeter guns, and a platform was erected on her trimmed afterdeck to accommodate a three-inch rifle. As soon as the extensive renovations were completed, custody of the vessel was transferred to the British Ministry of War Transport under the Lend Lease Act and she was moved to a convoy staging area in Newfoundland.

Escorted by His Majesty's Destroyers *Veteran* and *Vanoc* and in company with an Old Bay sister (the *Yorktown*) and six additional converted steamers, the *Warfield* set sail on September 20 from St. Johns, flying the Union Jack and bound for England and the grim business of war. She would encounter the latter all too soon.

In broad daylight on the afternoon of the fifth day out, the convoy commander's ship was struck by a torpedo and quickly sank. In the panic of evasive action, the steering gear of another vessel jammed; then a surfaced submarine was sighted along with two other periscopes. Convoy deck guns opened fire, and the British Admiralty would later credit the *Southland*, a thirty-four-year-old riverboat, with a probable kill.

During the melee, another torpedo was sighted, this one bearing down on *Warfield's* port beam. Quickly, her helmsman turned the boat into a parallel course, and the deadly fish passed with little more than thirty feet to spare. Action by the German wolf pack was proving a far hue and cry from the shot that had once been fired across her bow during Prohibition, when the Coast Guard had ordered her to halt for inspection, suspecting the packet of harboring a shipment of illicit whiskey.

Two minutes later, a submarine appeared close to *Warfield's* port quarter and her gunners opened fire. In response to frantic whistle signals, the destroyer *Veteran* joined the attack, unleashing a series of depth charges. It was the official consensus afterward that another of Hitler's U-boats would never return to its homeport.

A desperate, running battle continued throughout the day and a second steamer was torpedoed at dusk, exploding in a sheet of flame. Then, while picking up survivors, *H.M.S Veteran* was also struck and went down with a heavy loss of life.

On the evening of September 26, five hundred miles off the coast of Ireland, *Warfield's* former fleet mate, the *Yorktown*, became the final casualty of the ill-fated convoy. Hit amidships on the port side by a German torpedo, her superstructure collapsed and she slipped beneath the waves in less than three minutes.

The former pride of the Old Bay Line safely reached the coast of Devon and was moored at the town of Instow on the Torridge River. There she served as a training and barracks ship for British commandoes and marines until July, 1943, when she was transferred back to the U. S. Navy with the designation *U. S. S. President Warfield IX-169* and assigned as an assault-boat training base for American troops preparing for the invasion of Normandy.

I have read claims that D-Day landings of the 1st and 29th Divisions were accomplished under the direction of the *Warfield*, but sounder evidence indicates that she crossed the English Channel thirty days later and moored close to the artificial breakwater off Omaha Beach to serve as harbor control vessel and home for U.S. Navy personnel attached to the port director.

While wartime accommodations hardly compared to the luxurious suites she had offered during her Chesapeake packet days, the sailors who lived aboard were delighted with their assignment and gave her the nickname *U. S. S. Statler*. Curiously, one of her residents was I. J. Matacia, who was assigned to the same cabin he had shared with his wife on their honeymoon only a few years earlier.

When the ports of France finally opened to Allied shipping, *Warfield's* duties ended. She returned to England on November 13,

1944 and then briefly reappeared in France to serve on the Seine River, providing transportation between the towns of Le Havre and Rouen. Finally, unrecognizable to those who had known her glory days, she sailed back to the Chesapeake, arriving in Hampton Roads on July 25, 1945.

Decommissioned on September 19, the war-weary steamer was offered for sale. Her former owners checked her out but decided against the enormous expenditure it would have taken to refurbish her. When no other interests had materialized by November, she was towed to the Maritime Commission's idle fleet anchorage of surplus Liberty ships in the James River off Mulberry Island.

A year later, on November 11, 1946, the Potomac Shipwrecking Company of Washington paid $8,028 (some sources claim it was $6,255) for the hulk of the once palatial steamer. To the dismay of a generation of her fans, the *President Warfield* seemed headed toward an ignominious end on the scrap heap.

Two days later, however, the Potomac Company turned a tidy profit by transferring ownership of the rusting boat to the Weston Trading Company of New York for $40,000, and on February 2, 1947, a double-page pictorial spread in the Baltimore *Sun* carried the headline: "From Canton to Canton." The first Canton, of course, was a reference to Baltimore's commercial district, the second to Canton, China. The old packet, now under Honduran registry, was to be refitted and sailed to China to work out her days as a riverboat, the article announced.

British Intelligence officers watched closely as workers outfitted the boat at Portovenere, Italy. They followed when she sailed from Port-de-bouc and entered the harbor at Sète, France, where thousands of Jewish refugees—survivors of Hitler's Holocaust—had gathered from European detention centers.

Stanley Ritzer, a member of the ship's crew, later commented on the scene he witnessed as 4,554 displaced Jews packed on board the vessel that had been licensed for 540 passengers: "I stood at the top of the gangway as the refugees streamed onto the old ferry," Ritzer recalled. "There were old men, pregnant women, thin young men, beautiful girls, teenagers, infants. They all looked dirty, weary, hungry. Most of them wore all their clothes on their back and had the rest of their possessions in little bundles around their necks."

When the overcrowded vessel sailed on July 10, 1947, the British cruiser *H.M.S. Ajax* and a small fleet of destroyers gathered to shadow her. The entire world would soon know her name—*Exodus 1947*.

Palestine had been mandated to Great Britain at the end of World War I, and from the beginning the British found it difficult to manage relations between the province's resident Jews and its much larger Arab population. Now, with the Allied victory in World War II, tensions were running high as the Palestinian majority reacted angrily to an increased Jewish migration from war-torn Europe. To appease the Arabs, a determined British government tightened Jewish immigration quotas and sent Jews who ran their blockade to internment camps on the island of Cyprus.

Haganah, the military element of the Jewish underground, was equally committed to defending the provision in the mandate that called for a Jewish national home in Palestine. The stage was set for confrontation.

When it became clear that *Exodus 1947* was headed for Palestine, the commander of *Ajax* ordered her return to France, a directive ignored by the *Exodus* captain, who now proudly raised the blue and white flag of Zion.

As the jockeying vessels approached Palestinian waters in the dark, early morning hours of July 18, two British destroyers closed on *Exodus*, squeezing her from opposite sides. Gangplanks were dropped and fifty Royal Marines swarmed aboard the steamer in the face of a fusillade of hurled potatoes and tin cans, but the marines quickly cleared the decks with tear gas and clubs. Three Jews were killed during their fruitless resistance and another 217 injured.

"The ship looked like a matchbox that had been splintered by a nutcracker," wrote American journalist Ruth Gruber, who stood on a wharf in Haifa as *Exodus* limped into the harbor. "In the torn, square hole, as big as an open, blitzed barn, we could see a muddle of bedding, possessions, plumbing, broken pipes, overflowing toilets, half-naked men, women looking for children. Cabins were bashed in; railings were ripped off; the lifesaving rafts were dangling at crazy angles."

For the next several months, Gruber pursued the story, first to the prison camps on Cyprus, where she was misled by the British to believe they were sending the captured immigrants, then to France, where the Jews were actually transported and refused to disembark, and eventually to refugee camps in Hamburg, Germany. As the lone journalist covering the drama, Gruber's riveting dispatches and vivid photographs were circulated around the world, generating public sympathy for the Jewish refugees and a storm of disapproval against the British. Arguably, perhaps, they also influenced the United Nations decision to partition Palestine and establish the State of Israel in 1948.

Gruber's dispatches and photographs were collected in *Destination Palestine*, a book that became the basis for Leon Uris's best-selling novel *Exodus* and the popular movie of the same name, starring Paul Newman and Eva Marie Saint.

Upon the creation of the first Jewish state in the Holy Land since Nero's Roman armies had destroyed Jerusalem in 70 A.D., *Exodus 1947* became a special symbol of the Zionist struggle for sovereignty. Interest was strong for turning her into a museum, but requisites of the new nation and a war with surrounding Arab countries postponed the project.

For reasons that have never been discovered, *Exodus* caught fire at her moorings inside the breakwater of Haifa Harbor on the morning of August 26, 1952. Fireboats eventually brought the flames under control, but the steamer's superstructure had been destroyed. Soon afterward, she was towed to Kishon Harbor and sold to the Hayama Company for scrap.

So what is my point in telling you these apparently unrelated tales?

Remember the Weston Trading Company, the folks that sent the Chesapeake's beloved *President Warfield* off to China? The enterprise was never listed in a telephone or business directory. It occupied a shabby, one-room office on the fifth floor at 24 Stone Street in Manhattan. Weston was, in reality, a front for Haganah, and it was a group of Zionist sympathizers in Baltimore that paid the $40,000 to acquire the steamer.

The *President Warfield* never sailed to China; she crossed the Atlantic to Italy, instead, thence to France and Palestine. *President Warfield* became *Exodus 1947*, a gigantic symbol for a monumental cause and a legend that will live as long as Israel and its history survive.

Few tangible mementos of the *Warfield* remain. For years, the residents of Hagerstown, Maryland could set their clocks by the silver tones of her steam whistle, which was mounted on the roof of the New York Central Iron Works. Visitors to the Mariners Museum in Newport News can still hear the clang of her bell in the Chesapeake Bay Room.

Seldom has a ship seen so much history in such a brief time. "Her home port," wrote Alexander Crosby Brown, author of *Steam Packets on the Chesapeake*, "deservedly is Valhalla."

And there, as that other guy always says, you have the rest of the story.

Above: Exodus 1947 in Haifa Harbor, July 1947

Below: Exodus 1947 Burning in Haifa Harbor, August 26, 1952

On the Brink
of Change

The Eastern Shore in 1952

"All things must change," wrote Longfellow in Kèramos, "to something new, to something strange."

Fifty years. Half a century. To the young it represents an unimaginable eternity, while those of my age will tell you that it passes all too quickly, whether you are having fun or not.

In 1952 the United States was at war in Korea, and I spent the entire year in that theater of operations, adding a few service ribbons to my Air Force uniform. A century or two from now, those who scan records of Eastern Shore newspapers of the day will learn few details of our conflict with North Korea and China. They will discover little more than the names of some who left for the various services, where they trained and found assignment, when they returned—or if they did not. A constant reminder of the war's toll, however, was a weekly appeal in the press to donate blood for wounded soldiers.

If you craved battle news from Old Baldie, Pork Chop Hill, The Hook or Heartbreak Ridge, you listened to your radio or imported one of the city newspapers. A lucky few watched their television sets, which typically boasted a ten-inch screen, clouded by "snow" through all seasons. TV was still in its infancy, and when the

Tilghman Packing Company, distributors of seafood products, announced that for the first time in history a Talbot County product was being advertised regularly on TV, it made headlines in the *Star Democrat.*

January 1952 was considerably warmer than usual, the thermometer hitting a balmy 70 degrees on the 15th. Shortly after New Year's Day, the first set of "white triplets" ever recorded in Easton's Memorial Hospital was born to Mr. and Mrs. Sam Cohey of Queenstown. "Mother and youngsters doing fine," the paper reported. It was unusual to see someone identified as "white" in the press of that time, while African Americans were consistently identified as "Negro" or "colored."

"Louisiana Can't Find a Rat Skinner to Give Battle to Maryland," a February 1 headline shouted. "Louisiana may have more muskrats than Maryland, but Maryland has better skinners," the text continued. "This was proved today in the announcement that no one has come forth from the southern state to accept battle with a skinner from Maryland." Representative Edward Miller had issued an unanswered challenge to Louisiana Representative Henry Larcade to send a muskrat skinner to compete in the annual outdoor show at Cambridge.

On another cold February day, the Easton Coca-Cola Bottling Company was touting a six-bottle carton of its product for 25¢ plus deposit. "Thirst knows no season—nor does ice-cold Coca-Cola," the ad announced.

Tarbutton's, "The Lady's Quality Shop," was selling winter dresses for $3-$4 each and winter hats for $1, while Bata had jumped the season by offering new summer styles in hosiery at 69¢ each or $2 for a box of three.

At The Men's Shop you could outfit your son in a long-sleeved flannel shirt for 98¢, a long-sleeved T-shirt for 49¢, an all-wool topcoat for $9.95, an all-wool suit for $12.95 and blue denim dungarees or raincoat for 98¢. Men's all wool suits and topcoats were listed at $19.95 and sport coats at $14.95, topped off with a hat for $3.95.

At Reeds' "Dollar Sale," a dozen large-size men's handkerchiefs, an 8-cup percolator or a polished aluminum roaster cost $1, but 5-piece knife and cleaver sets, pocket watches and alarm clocks were included in the ad for $2, and a solid brass 3-way lamp with shade for $3.

A bed with headboard and quality hotel innerspring mattress and matching box spring was published on sale for $69.50. Replacing your icebox with a "family-sized Frigidaire" strained one's finances at $199.75, but there were more than a few Eastern Shore homes that were not yet equipped with electricity to operate one. Parking a new automobile in your garage really tested the budget at $1,000, give or take a little. It was more affordable to outfit the old car with "tough, long-wearing Goodyear tires with safe, new Goodyear treads" at $10.05 per wheel.

At the A&P you could buy a can of cat food for 8¢. Lifesavers were three rolls for a dime, as were packs of chewing gum. An eight-ounce box of Corn Flakes or Wheaties set you back 16¢, while 19¢ bought a package of cookies, a #1 can of peaches, a bottle of tomato catsup, two ounces of stuffed olives or a roll of Scottowels. Six, five-cent candy bars (and do you remember how big they were) sold for a quarter. A can of tuna or a pound of margarine added 23¢ to your tab at checkout. Orange juice brought 21¢ for a 46-ounce can. Two, one-pound tins of pork and beans could be yours for 23¢, while single cans of sweet peas and golden corn rang up 19¢ on the register. You were charged 29¢ a pound for pork loin roast, 45¢ for smoked picnic ham and 65¢ for lean smoked ham. Turkey growers had not yet discovered the secrets of mass production, and their product claimed a whopping 71¢ per pound. Large Florida oranges commanded 25¢ a dozen or 49¢ for two dozen. Oysters were listed at 75¢ a pint or 85¢ for select, and fancy shrimp brought 59¢ a pound. The Acme held a "gigantic sale" on "juicy Florida grapefruit," four for 19¢, and sold California lemons for 39¢ a dozen.

Those who were creative with their pens vied in an essay contest to share their "favorite way to use Sweetheart Bread," the winner to be treated to a $50 grocery-shopping spree by the Sweetheart Bakers of Salisbury.

In March, a storm destroyed many trees and power lines, and a man was lost in the Bay.

A large photograph of Miss Ruth Ferrick, holding a two-headed tulip discovered by Mrs. Jean Grant of the Eastern Shore Nurseries, made Page 1 news, as did the crowning of Sylvia Jarboe of Sherwood as Miss Miles River, "amid festivities as gay, as colorful, as exciting as the crowning of any princess, anywhere."

It was astounding to many that fifteen years after the inauguration of the Federal Old Age and Survivors Insurance program (Social Security) $2,000,000 a year was being paid in benefits to men, women and children on the Eastern Shore of Maryland and Virginia. Less space was given to the report that 545 people had died during 1951 on Maryland highways.

"An attractive town house in a very desirable location on the south end of Easton" with four bedrooms, basement, furnace and "nice-sized lot" was advertised at $14,000. Or perhaps you would have preferred a living room, dining room, modern kitchen, four bedrooms and bath, with venetian blinds, sanded and finished floors, large fenced lot and garage (location not stated) for $7,400. A double, twelve-room house on a large lot was listed at $10,000.

A "nice farm" of 136 acres, 80 tillable, with marketable timber, a six-room and bath house "in prime condition," an 18,000-capacity broiler house, barn, milk house and other outbuildings, fenced pasture bordering a stream, new tractor, accessories and other equipment could have been yours for $35,000, while a smaller homestead of 37 acres with a six-room house, two barns and other outbuildings was available for $8,000.

Had you been in the market to combine the serenity of waterfront living with a little farming, 48 acres along 1,500 feet of deep water, a four-bedroom house plus tenant house, a hundred–foot chicken house and other outbuildings in St. Michaels carried an asking price of $31,500.

Need to do a little landscaping or road work on your property? Sand fill and gravel was being delivered for $5 a load, $4 each for ten loads or more. Dirt, gravel and oyster-shell thoroughfares were still common throughout the Shore.

In rural areas, which then comprised nearly all of Delmarva, entertainment focused on the radio and gatherings in country stores and private homes, while in town, motion pictures packed in the crowds. Theater patrons rolled in the aisles over the antics of Abbott and Costello in *Jack and the Beanstalk*, *The Naughty Nineties* and *Little Giant*; Dean Martin and Jerry Lewis in *Sailor Beware*; and Leo Gorcey and the Bowery Boys in *Ghost Chasers* and *Let's Go Navy*.

Western fans found plenty of fare to choose from, including Randolph Scott and Broderick Crawford in *When the Daltons Rode*, James Stewart and Rock Hudson in *Bend of the River*, Glenn Ford and Rhonda Flemming in *Redhead and the Cowboy*, and Gene Autrey in *Apache Country*.

And there were sagas of war, musicals, comedies and dramas aplenty. Audie Murphy, the most decorated American soldier in World War II, shared the lead in *Raging Tide* with Shelly Winters. William Holden starred in *Boots Malone* and in *Submarine Command* with William Bendix. Doris Day and Danny Thomas made *I'll See You in My Dreams* memorable. Gene Nelson, Virginia Mayo and Dennis Morgan entertained in *Painting the Clouds with Sunshine*, and Shelly Winters, Gary Merrill, Michael Rennie, Kenin Wynn and Betty Davis held us spellbound in *Phone Call from a Stranger*. Merrill and Davis also starred in *Another Man's Poison*, and Broderick Crawford traded in his cowboy boots to join Donna Reed and John Derrick in *The Scandal Sheet*. Jane Russell was *His Kind of Woman* with Robert Mitchum and also paired with Victor Mature in *The Las Vegas Story*. Tony Curtis joined Piper Laurie to play *The Prince Was a Thief*. Susan Hayward and Rory Calhoon lifted everyone's spirits *With a Song in My Heart*. Burt Lancaster had the lead in *Ten Tall Men*, Humphrey Bogart and Ethel Barrimore in *Deadline-U.S.*, Errol Flynn and Ruth Roman in *Mara Maru*, Frederick March in *Death of a Salesman*, John Wayne and Ann Dvorak in *Flame of the Barbary Coast*, Ester Williams in *Skirts Ahoy* and Tony Curtis in *Flesh and Fury*.

In that memorable year for Hollywood, *Snow White and the Seven Dwarfs* made one of what would become a long line of comebacks, and moviegoers everywhere scanned the posters and theater marquis for those enticing words: "Color by Technicolor."

Cinema fans would have to wait until March 19, 1953 to learn that *The Greatest Show on Earth* had triumphed over *High Noon, Ivanhoe, Moulin Rouge* and *The Quiet Man* for best motion picture, and that Gary Cooper had surpassed Marlon Brando, Kirk Douglas, Josè Ferrer and Alex Guinness as best actor for his performance in *High Noon.* Shirley Booth, in *Come Back Little Sheba,* beat out perennial contenders Joan Crawford, Betty Davis, Julie Harris and Susan Hayward for best actress, and Anthony Quinn in *Viva Zapata* and Gloria Grahame in *The Bad and the Beautiful* were named top achievers in supporting roles.

And Hollywood came to Delmarva in 1952. "Dana Andrews and Louise Allbritton, two bright stars," the *Star Democrat* announced, "will float from the sky and land at the Easton Airport on May 24 for their top rolls in the duPont Company's 'Cavalcade of America' broadcast," which was held at Seaford on May 27. The actors stayed at the Tidewater Inn in Easton.

With a starting salary of $2,000 and a high of $3,800, Talbot County's 126 teachers were averaging $3,431 for a year's work, while 13 principals received slightly more than $4,000. In an address on the Eastern Shore, Governor Theodore R. McKeldin declared that it was morally wrong for the state to dole out salary increases to teachers. "I will continue to veto any bill for teacher salary increases by the state," he threatened. In April, county commissioners granted the educators a $300 annual raise.

On April 25, an air force plane flying from Andrews Air Force Base to Boston crashed six miles north of Easton in a rainstorm, killing the pilot, Colonel Robert Leary. The wreckage was strewn over 50 acres, and Leary's helmet was found a quarter of a mile away. The plane went into a steep dive, J. E. Hogue of Wye Mills reported, and the combined force of the crash and the explosion tore a huge hole in the rain-soaked field at the edge of a wooded area.

Heavy rains in May caused severe damage to the Shore's strawberry crop, and the world's largest frying pan was already drawing visitors to the Delmarva Chicken Festival, which was held on June 9 and 10 at Pocomoke City. 5,000 had swarmed over the pan the year before in Salisbury, papers announced, and ate 2,300 pounds of fried chicken in a few minutes. It was promised that the chefs would have a larger supply of fowl on hand in '52.

Oystermen, oyster packers, sportsmen, realtors and legislators met with the director of the State Health Department to discuss the growing threat of pollution to state oyster-producing waters. One of the chief causes of concern cited was the overboard discharge of waste by boatmen. "All other known sources of sewage disposal into these bodies of water have been checked," the group claimed.

"Will Talbot County be next?" the *Star Democrat* asked as summer approached. "Will the county commissioners wait until rabies cases develop before enforcing the dog licensing law or setting up a quarantine for all dogs found on the loose?" Counties north of the Chesapeake and Delaware Canal and the town of Seaford had recently been placed under a dog quarantine. "The time to take these steps right here at home in Talbot County is now," admonished the Easton newspaper, "not after someone has been infected from the bite or even the playful lick of a dog."

Spraying to control flies, mosquitoes and other insects was scheduled monthly from May through September. "In view of the fact it appears that flies and mosquitoes have to a very considerable extent become immune to DDT and in line with the views of Dr. George S. Lankford, specialist in insect control of the University of Maryland," a news bulletin informed us, "nine gallons of 11% of BHC will be used in each 125 gallon mixture. There will be a little odor to the mixture but it will be short lived." The same page carried the headline: "Cancer Crusade 13% Above Goal."

The Mule
That Wrote a Book

A t the southernmost tip of Talbot County, a few hundred yards east of the Frederick C. Malkus Bridge and Choptank River Fishing Pier, Bolingbroke Creek slews around a sandbar and broadly cleaves its way into the fertile countryside. To focus alone on the aspect of the creek's mouth and its immediate fringe is to view the river much as it must have appeared when only wind and waterfowl, schools of breaking fish and Indian dugouts disturbed its sweeping tides. When the Choptank sprawls as still as a mirror and dawn mists wreathe the Talbot headland, there is no lovelier scene anywhere on the Delmarva Peninsula.

Early in the twentieth century, before the construction of the Harrington Bridge, which is now the fishing pier, a hunting lodge stood on the western shore of Bolingbrook Creek on a plantation familiarly known as Cambridge Ferry Farm. As was customary with any such enterprise before the age of mechanization, an assortment of animals found employment there in the cultivation and harvesting of crops, and among the Ferry Farm livestock, one beast—a mule named Pete—stood conspicuously above his peers for beauty, intelligence and remarkable character.

Pete was a mule of medium size, dark in color and with a light marking around his muzzle. He had a broad forehead, brilliant eyes,

Pete, the Mule That Wrote a Book

and though possessed of a fine disposition, was not too proud to defend his dignity as only a mule can. But above all, it is claimed, Pete was intelligent to a startling degree.

As the men talked and planned their work for the following day, Pete always appeared to be listening, and if some difficult task was suggested, the mule was often absent in the morning. Pete would simply jump the fence during the night, it was assumed, and go off to another farm. Everybody knew the animal and thought a great deal of him, and he was always well treated by the neighbors. As a result of these frequent disappearances, it was accepted without question that Pete understood what was being said and made himself scarce to avoid the hard work.

Those who knew the Eastern Shore "before the bridge" will remember the simple delights of life in those times and the happy atmosphere that surrounded the gathering of friends for games and entertainment and especially for the sharing of stories. Pete not only employed his humanistic traits to the end of avoiding work, but he listened to the tales told around the lodge and eventually published his favorite observations in a book—*Bolingbroke Lodge: Some Short Stories and Some Serious Thoughts.*

"I was born in the Ozark Mountains in the State of Missouri," Pete began. "Perhaps because of the place of my nativity I could never take anything for granted. My father had a very unfortunate name [his father, of course, was an ass] so I came east looking for work. By good fortune I found employment on this farm on the Eastern Shore of Maryland in Talbot County, bordering upon the bay of the Choptank River and on Bolingbroke Creek. Here I have worked, single, for nearly twenty-five years, cultivating corn, raking hay and performing general agricultural tasks. I love this country and have always been treated with fair consideration.

"During my residence here, many persons have visited this locality for hunting and fishing and for general recreation. Folks of varied occupations, industrialists and professionals, have come from the North as well as from the South, all seeking sport and health and finding both in abundance. While working at my occupations, I have listened carefully to what they have said and treasure what I have heard. I have thought it over, digested it mentally and meditated upon it in silence while performing my many lines of work.

"We are all vain—some more, others less—so I have had my picture printed at the front of this little book in the hope that someone in the future may remember me. We must all pass on from this life into the next, and happy indeed is the individual who leaves a memory, as the rose leaves its sweet fragrance."

My favorite of the stories Pete collected at Bolingbroke Lodge is of an earnest Christian man who had a reputation as an eloquent preacher. Of one sermon, "And Then There Was Daniel," he was especially proud. As with the preceding quotes from Pete, I have taken a few liberties with editing.

"When Daniel came out of the land of Canaan" Pete's version begins, "he was scared and hard pressed, and he fell among thieves. One thief hit him with a blackjack and another cut him four times with a razor and left him for dead.

"Just about that time a good Samaritan came riding by on a hide-bound mule. He rolled Daniel over on one side, washed his wounds with corn liquor, put him up on the mule and took him into town. The good Samaritan dumped Daniel off at the front gate of King Nebuchadnezzar, the same what eat grass like a cow. No more than he took him into the presence of the great King Nebuchadnezzar, the same what eat grass like a cow, Daniel fell down before the great king and said. 'Oh, King Nebuchadnezzar, live forever, live forever!'

"But King Nebuchadnezzar, the same what eat grass like a cow, said, 'Hist yourself up, Daniel, and tell me how come you got beated up like this.'

"Daniel said, 'Oh, King Nebuchadnezzar, I fell among thieves and am sick and hard pressed. I welcome any little rest you can give me.'

"King Nebuchadnezzar, the same what eat grass like a cow, said, 'Daniel, what you do for a living?'

"And Daniel replied, 'Oh, King Nebuchadnezzar, I is an architect, but the bad times done got me down.'

"Then King Nebuchadnezzar, the same what eat grass like a cow, said, 'Daniel, if you am an architect, I want you to build me a palace. I want it to be the bestest palace in all the land of the kingdom. I want you to spare no expense. I don't care if you spend $500 for it. I am going to assign you to Room 401 for your room and Room 402 for your working room, but under no excuse must you open the window and look toward Jerusalem.'

"So Daniel went up to Room 401, and he pulled off his shoes, and he got the gravel out from between his toes, and it was right warm in Room 401. Daniel had not had anything to eat, and he began to think about Jerusalem and all those good chitterlings, cracklings and fried fish there. Finally, he opened up the window and gave the high sign salute towards Jerusalem.

"Just about that time, a chambermaid bringing a slop jar and some fresh water opened the door, but seeing Daniel, she slammed the door and ran down the stairs and fell before King Nebuchadnezzar, the same what eat grass like a cow, and said, 'Oh, King Nebuchadnezzar, live forever, live forever!'

"Whereupon King Nebuchadnezzar, the same what eat grass like a cow, said, 'Hist yourself up gal and tell me what's on your mind.'

"She said, 'Oh, King Nebuchadnezzar, I have been a chambermaid four years and three months in this here palace. I am a hard-working woman trying to feed a worthless husband and four childrens, and here's this man Daniel in Room 401 with the window open, letting all that dust come in for me to clean up.'

"So King Nebuchadnezzar, the same what eat grass like a cow, sent for Daniel, and he said, 'Look a-here, Daniel, I done told you once not to open that window and look toward Jerusalem. Now I tells you twice times. Go back to your room and start to build that palace I told you about.'

"So Daniel went back to Room 401 and laid his head on his knees. By and by he heard somebody on the street below calling, 'Watermelons, watermelons,' and Daniel opened the window and looked right in the face of the tax collector.

"The tax collector wheeled directly in the palace gate and fell down before King Nebuchadnezzar, the same what eat grass like a cow, and he said, 'Oh, King Nebuchadnezzar, live forever, live forever!'

"And the great king histed him up and told him to say his say.

"The tax collector said, 'Oh, King, I am your faithful servant. I collect your taxes and listen to the growls of your people, but here I look up this morning, and there in Room 401 is that man Daniel with the window open, letting in all the cold air, and the people paying good money to heat this here palace and keep it warm. It's enough to make them all go out and vote the Democratic ticket.'

"So King Nebuchadnezzar, the same what eat grass like a cow, sent for Daniel again and said, 'Daniel, I done told you once, I done told you twice, and I tells you again about opening that window and looking toward Jerusalem. I hears you am a wise man and a prophet, so now I gives you one more chance. I been having a heap of bad dreams and can't do no good sleeping nights. Now tell me about these dreams and I'll save you from being thrown in the lions' den.'

"And Daniel said, Oh, King, live forever, live forever! You dream bad dreams for two reasons: The first is cause you got a burden on your stummik, and the second is cause you got a burden on your soul. The first is from eating too much green corn and pork chops, and the second is cause you threw them three boys, Meshack, Shadrack and Abednego into the fiery furnace. But oh, King, live forever!'

"And it came to pass that this made King Nebuchadnezzar, the same what eat grass like a cow, hopping mad, and he called his overseer named Belshazzar, and he says, 'I stands no more foolishments from this man Daniel. Throw him in the lions' den.'

"So Belshazzar took Daniel by the hand and led him out of the presence of the great King Nebuchadnezzar, the same what eat grass like a cow, and took him into the big tent, and as they entered the big tent, Belshazzar led him between three rings and multitudes of peoples. The elephant snorted at Daniel, the trapeze man kicked him as he looped the loop, the Hittites hit him with peanuts, and the Pharisees flung popcorn at him, but Daniel was not afraid.

"And then they come to the lions' den, all painted red and gold and on four big red wheels, and Belshazzar pushed Daniel right up to the door of the lions' den. There was four lions in there, two little ones and two big ones, and their names was writted in handwriting on the wall. The two little ones was named Mene and Mene, and the two big ones was Tekel and Upharsin.

"And then he shoved Daniel right plumb in the lions' den.

"The two little lions walked up to one side of Daniel and said, 'G-r-r-ruw.'

"The two big lions walked up to the other side of Daniel and said, 'Gru-r-o-o-w,' but Daniel was not afraid.

"And Daniel looked at the little lions, and then he looked at the big lions, and Daniel said, 'Scat out of here, you African cats, and go on about your business.'

"And all those lions went over in the corner and laid down and begun licking their whiskers with their paws.

"Now, brethren and sistern, the point I makes is who saved Daniel from the lions' den? Who closed the lions' mouth and locked his teeth? Who makes the corn grow tall and the sweet taters big and yellow? Who puts the fat on the possum and the kink in his tail? Who was this man?

"I tells you, brethren, he was the greatest man in the land of Canaan and the land of cotton. I tells you who he is: He is no other than ABRAHAM WASHINGTON FRANKLIN LINCOLN. Looking back over the untrodden paths of the future, we behold the footprints of the hand of the Almighty."

Justus A. B. Cowles is assumed to have assisted Pete in his literary venture, and in 1937, Mr. Cowles distributed the privately published and very limited edition of *Bolingbroke Lodge* to his friends with Christmas greetings and best wishes for the New Year.

So here's to your memory, Pete, may it linger as long as the sweet fragrance of the rose. Every time I cross the Choptank River on Senator Fred's bridge, I shall glance up the graceful curve of Bolingbroke Creek and think of you.

Postscript: I never believed there would be anyone alive who had actually known Pete, so imagine my surprise when I received the following letter shortly after this story appeared in *Tidewater Times*.

Dear Hal,

When there was not enough to eat at my home in Oxford in 1933, I went to live with my Uncle Bowdle Highley on Cambridge Ferry Farm. He had a big house and lots of food.

My uncle had five farms between the Choptank River and Trappe. One day I wished to shoot rabbits on the Beaver Dam Farm, where the greatest concentration of rabbits existed. Since Pete the mule was the only transportation available to me, I rode him while holding my gun.

I had a successful shoot, and since Pete was so slow, I decided to cut through the woods. That proved to be a mistake because Pete decided to go his route instead of mine, and for a good reason. He found a tree that had a very low limb, and then he showed the first speed of the day. He passed under the limb at full speed and wiped me off onto the ground. I was scratched up and a little sore from the fall. I never caught up with Pete, so when I came to a house, I gave the rabbits away. I never rode Pete through the woods again.

When summer came and school was out, Uncle Bowdle teamed me up with Pete for the various jobs around the farm. Pete never teamed up with another mule. He was an individual. Certain jobs he seemed to like. One was pulling a load of hay up to the loft. He didn't like the hay rake or cultivating corn. He seemed to step on the corn on purpose, but we would do it from sunup to almost sundown.

I talked to Pete all day long. We both fought the horse flies and sheep flies, and by the end of the week we were both fed up with the job. I decided I wanted a day off, so during the night I slipped over to the fenced-in area where the mules were kept. Pete recognized me and came to the gate immediately. I opened the gate enough for him to slip out. Then I fastened the gate and quickly slipped back into my bed.

The next morning Pete was gone. Whenever I needed a day off, I repeated this maneuver. Pete gained quite a reputation for understanding when the men were planning to work him hard the next day and jumping the fence that night to avoid work.

Mr. Cowles, a lawyer from Rye, New York, who built the hunting lodge in which my uncle and aunt lived, extolled the cleverness of Pete. His many guests always had to go to see Pete and hear about how smart he was. He brought Dr. Bird, an anthropologist from the New York Museum of Natural History, who studied him for three days. He even had the farmer talk about a strenuous job for Pete the next day. That night Pete left the farm. This was all recorded in Dr. Bird's notes.

Finally, Mr. Cowles wrote a little blue book about Pete. There was more Canadian Club drunk discussing Pete than he was worth. After all, Pete's father was an ass. In retrospect, Pete made asses of a lot of people from Rye, New York, who thought they were very smart.

Sincerely.
Fletcher Hanks

Many will recognize the name of Fletcher Hanks, a Talbot County native whose writings and adventures are well known on the Eastern Shore. As a young man during World War II, Hanks flew for the China National Aviation Corporation.

When the Burma Road, China's last connection to the sea, was cut by Japanese forces, CNAC air freighters were forced to fly over the Himalayan ranges to continue the flow of vital supplies. If you draw a graph of the flight path, showing elevation changes from one end to the other, it looks exactly like the hump of a camel, and so it came to be known as "flying The Hump." During three and a half years, 800,000 tons of war material and 33,500 personnel were transported in small cargo planes over The Hump, totaling 1.5 million hours of flying time.

As the route flew over mountains exceeding 20,000 feet in elevation, glaciers, tropical rainforests and regions occupied by the Japanese Army, Hump pilots had to endure the most severe weather conditions and some of the most challenging and dangerous flying of the war. 563 planes went down on The Hump—many in the sights of Japanese fighter planes—with a loss of more than 1,500 Chinese and American pilots and crewmembers. The Hump is considered by some to have been the greatest challenge and the greatest tragedy in aviation history.

Fletcher Hanks flew The Hump more than 900 times and has returned to Asia on several occasions, even as a septuagenarian, to aid in the continuing search for some of the crash sites.

The Last Wild River

There are objects in nature—rocks, the best example—that demonstrate little visible or physical change over a period of many years. Alteration for most things is effected through a process of gradual transition; in other words, change usually takes time—maybe a little, maybe a lot, but it takes time. Rivers are an exception. Like the wind, a river changes every second. This, of course, is what Heraclitus had in mind when he said that you cannot step twice into the same river.

Since time immemorial, men have followed rivers for a great variety of reasons. The incentive has often been economic, but adventure has just as frequently been the goal. In 1541, Francisco de Orellani made the inaugural descent of the Amazon from the Andes to the Atlantic, battling the Tapuyan Indians along the way. Then, in 1638, Pedro Teixeira became the first to cover the same route in reverse. I assume they each did so for the hell of it—because the river was there to follow.

Cataracts, diverging branches, wild animals and nearly impenetrable wilderness impeded those who searched for the source of the Nile for centuries. H. M. Stanley surmounted some of those obstacles in 1875, only to be turned back by threats of war. While most of the secrets of the Nile have since been unraveled, there remain challenges aplenty between the Mediterranean Sea and the headwaters of its major tributaries.

But one need not journey to the far reaches of the earth to experience an epic river adventure. At age sixty-seven, Colin Fletcher, the guru of backpacking in America, made a six-month, single-handed, foot-and-raft expedition down the one-thousand-seven-hundred-mile length of the Colorado, beginning beside a trickle of water in the mountains of Wyoming and ending at the Gulf of California. He is probably the only person to have ever accomplished that feat. Why did he do it? In *River*, published in 1997, he said it was because he needed "something to pare the fat off my soul...to make me grateful, again, for being alive."

Indeed, there is something compelling about rivers and some power within them that cleanses the soul and joins one closer with the earth. Rivers carry the lifeblood of the earth, and there is a river near enough for each of us to know and to follow.

In 1941, when I was ten years old, a friend of my father retired and moved from our Pennsylvania community to Sharptown, Maryland. Throughout the remaining decade of my growing up, I looked forward to Al Leh's occasional trips north. If his visit happened to coincide with the hunting season, he generally brought a brace of wild ducks for our table. Watermelons and cantaloupes rolled from the trunk of his car in the warmer months. But of far more interest to me, this hero of my youth always appeared armed with a new story about his adventures on a tidal waterway that he had come to love. Whenever people ask me how I happen to be living near the Nanticoke River, I tell them it's Al Leh's fault.

The Nanticoke River begins its life in a multitude of small branches and ditches in the heart of the Sussex County countryside northeast of Seaford, Delaware, the site where practical navigation ends, but its power surges from the tides of Chesapeake Bay and the Atlantic Ocean beyond. It is connected, as are all rivers, to the pulse of the planet.

Sometimes referred to as Delmarva's last wild river, the Nanticoke is a beautiful and mostly secluded waterway, with the majority of its thirty-six serpentine miles forming the boundary between the

Maryland counties of Dorchester and Wicomico. Winding gently to the southwest, its ever-broadening flow empties into Tangier Sound, where it shares an expansive mouth with the Wicomico and Monie Rivers to the east and Fishing Bay to the west.

From Seaford and Woodland—in Delaware—past Galestown, Sharptown and historic Vienna—in Maryland—pine forests, swampy cripples and sloughs dominate the river shore. Then, after Vienna and a few farmlands are left behind, the great Dorchester marshes prevail to the western horizon, while along the eastern bank one encounters less expansive wetlands and the placid waterfront communities of Tyaskin, Bivalve and Nanticoke.

On Delmarva's last wild river you will encounter no white-water challenges, no thundering cataracts to impede your journey, no headhunters propelling poisoned darts, nor (if you discount the growing number of weekend speed boats and jet-skis) any dangerous beasts, but for me it is no less a well of mystery and adventure.

As incorrect as they have been, I am grateful to people like Paul Wilstach, who wrote in his once popular *Tidewater Maryland* (1931): "On Nanticoke there is little of historical interest. During the Revolutionary War a British gunboat, in what would seem to have been a particularly idle moment, ascended the river and threw shots into the town [Vienna]. In the second war with England other British gunboats came within sight of the town but, with a truer sense of economy, did not throw any shots." Wilstach left out so much.

I am grateful to Fessenden S. Blanchard and Robert F. Duncan, who had this to say about the Nanticoke in *A Cruising Guide to the Chesapeake* (1950): "Unless you like low featureless marshland and narrow channels between extensive shoals, there is very little to appeal to the yachtsman on Nanticoke River." Obviously, Blanchard and Duncan never journeyed far beyond the river's mouth.

I am even more grateful to people like Ken Carter who, in his boat and bike journey, *Chesapeake Reflections* (1991), ignored the Nanticoke completely.

I feel indebted to all the writers who have scorned one of the Chesapeake Bay's most unique river systems, and by so doing may have contributed to the maintenance of its relatively unspoiled condition. But to continue now to ignore it could mean its destruction. It is time to shout about the Nanticoke's charm and wildness in the hope that it is not too late to keep it that way. We have already witnessed the beginning of deterioration.

From colonial times into the twentieth century, the American shad was the dominant fishery of the Nanticoke River, but its population has been so severely decimated through over fishing, reduction of water quality and the damming of many tributaries that few people under the age of forty have ever seen one, and its numbers have dropped below the threshold where it can replenish itself.

To help shad populations rebound, both Maryland and Delaware have been experimenting with small hatcheries. Eggs are removed from migrating females caught in the Nanticoke and fertilized with milt from males also taken from the river. Until they reach a growth stage where they stand a fair chance of survival in the wild, shad fry are held in a controlled environment.

State departments in Delaware and Maryland, agencies of the federal government and organizations such as the Nanticoke Watershed Alliance, the Chesapeake Bay Foundation, the Nature Conservancy and the Conservation Fund are working to restore and retain the natural character and health of this irreplaceable resource, and it is time for other government agencies as well as developers and individual landowners to start the wheels rolling for the removal or bypass of the numerous obstructions in Nanticoke tributaries that have cut off many of the traditional spawning grounds for shad and herring. The job will not be easy, nor will it ever be completed.

Lisa Jo Frech, founding Executive Director of the Nanticoke Watershed Alliance, a bi-state effort of more than thirty organizations to conserve the river, once said to me: "Everywhere I go, I say that this river doesn't know state boundaries and it doesn't know county boundaries. That's a ridiculous concept, and as long as we think of it as Maryland's portion and Delaware's portion, Dorchester's side and Wicomico's side, we'll never be doing the river any favor. As a country and as a world we need to be thinking about watersheds. All of our planning and zoning and education should be focused on watersheds."

Quite correct, but more easily uttered than accomplished. Too many politicians will continue to play...well...politics, and too many people who hold deeds to real estate will continue to believe that they should have the right to do whatever they choose with the land, regardless of the impact on others and on the environment.

Waterfront property has escalated enormously in value. In addition to the historic attraction for industrial and recreational interests, living on the water—any water—has become a romantic idyll. Where the landscape bordering waterways has proven unsuitable for home sites or marinas or power plants, men have traditionally sought to drain or fill or modify it in some manner to make it so. We have recognized that a large portion of the Nanticoke's shoreline consists of wetland—marsh and swampy woods. So far, these riparian features have helped to protect the river from excessive development, but in view of our burgeoning population and sprawling suburbia, the Nanticoke is no longer very remote, nor is its topography excessively challenging for today's developer.

Timber is money also, and frequently on Delmarva it has been viewed as the only practical source of income from forests growing on or bordering our wetlands. The fact that these woodland buffers, by preventing erosion and trapping or absorbing pollutants, are critical to the health of the river is a relatively recent understanding. Even when it is clearly in our favor to retain these natural bulwarks, it is sometimes difficult to overcome traditional views of economics and accept the fact that changing times require changing attitudes and tactics.

The Chesapeake Bay Foundation's Nanticoke Watershed Initiative is striving to protect and maintain the pristine nature of the river, while at the same time encouraging sustainable economic development. I asked Don Jackson when he was the Nanticoke Project Manager for CBF how you do that.

"You have to get people to recognize and understand," he explained, "that the natural resources in the region are the most valuable commodity of the economy, and that if you trash those resources in the name of traditional economic development, you will end up eroding your economic base and be faced with all kinds of problems down the road—a polluted river and economics that are not sustainable in the long run.

"On the other hand, if you are able to maintain the integrity of the watershed and the natural resources in the watershed and grow the economy around those resources in ways that don't harm them, it will allow you to maintain the economic base and make your overall economy that much stronger."

There are always a few people that will put personal interests ahead of environmental considerations and even the law. Perhaps the most flagrant violator on the Nanticoke in recent years has been Edwin H. Lewis, a retired Tommy Hilfiger executive.

In 1999, Mr. Lewis purchased sixty acres of marsh along the shores of the Nanticoke in Wicomico County. The property, a few miles downriver from the town of Vienna, included a five-acre, forested island, ninety-five percent of which was protected from development by the Maryland Critical Area Act of 1984, a landmark law and the cornerstone of legislation to preserve the remaining natural shoreline of the Chesapeake and its tributaries, which is critical to preserving water quality and wildlife. Almost immediately and with total disregard for the act or Wicomico County building and zoning laws, Lewis engaged a contractor to erect a six-building, hunting lodge complex on the island.

Construction in the isolated area was seventy-five percent completed before it came to the attention of county officials, who ordered Mr. Lewis to halt the work and remove the buildings. His response was to appeal for a variance.

Although Lewis insisted that he had destroyed only a couple live trees and perhaps a dozen dead or dying ones, a representative of the Chesapeake Bay Foundation visited the island and counted more than a hundred stumps of large, healthy trees, many of them hidden from general view in the crawl spaces of buildings.

At a meeting of the Wicomico County Board of Zoning Appeals on October 11, 2000, Lisa Jo Frech was among the crowd of concerned citizens who came to urge board members to uphold the law. Although her remarks were addressed to the board, she turned to face Lewis as she spoke.

"I've tried very hard to think about this case without taking into consideration the fact that Mr. Lewis ordered all the construction without obtaining any permits. Should he be granted an exception within the critical area for a private venture? No amount of mental wrangling can produce a fair answer to this question because it is a question out of context. The point is that Mr. Lewis ignored numerous county and state laws for personal gain.

"Mr. Lewis has been associated with the Shore long enough to make some friends here, but not long enough to realize that some of those friends are friends of ours. He has been quoted as saying some very derogatory things about the people of Wicomico County and of the Eastern Shore. Some of the people he has spoken to in this manner would gladly testify to that fact if that were required. But it should not be necessary. It's also not necessary to debate whether or not Mr. Lewis knew what he was doing. One doesn't become a CEO of a large and successful company without some shrewdness. By his actions and in his words, Mr. Lewis has taken us for simple fools, and he believes that with enough money and time he will get at least some of what he has intended for his property on the Nanticoke. If it weren't for these actions, very few of us would be here tonight. It is the intention of his actions that is unprecedented and must be addressed.

"It is unfortunate that there is nothing on the books in reference to permits and exceptions after the fact. Perhaps after tonight we will change that, in which case we will owe thanks to Mr. Lewis for prompting us to prepare for other blatant violators.

"Many eyes are watching us tonight. Somerset County has a similar case, which they have put on hold in order to see what decision we make. Planners at the state level are watching. Concerned citizens are here tonight from other watersheds on the Shore who care very much about this case. Everyone knows that this will be a landmark case, an example for the Shore and potentially for the Chesapeake Bay.

"I've not heard from one person that Mr. Lewis should be allowed to do whatever he wants with his property. Citizens all around the bay have had to adhere to these laws. They haven't been very cheerful about it. They've sacrificed personal dreams, but they have complied for the benefit of the Chesapeake Bay, a place they proudly call home. If any compromise is made with Mr. Lewis, the message will be clear: 'Wicomico County is a pushover.'

"The Nanticoke River is one of the two cleanest rivers that flow into the Chesapeake Bay. We've known that now for ten years. If we can't draw a line and show some backbone to people who blatantly ignore county and state laws that were designed to protect our environmental health and legacy, then the Chesapeake Bay will surely go down the toilet, and all of us with it.

"The Wicomico County Board of Zoning Appeals' decision on this case will be a turning point in history, no matter which way it goes. The decision made by this board will be a precedent referenced by many for years to come. This is no small matter. The future of the Nanticoke River, the Lower Shore and beyond will be determined by what happens here tonight. The choices are to open the floodgates for more of these illegal actions or put a stop to them right now. The citizens of this county are counting on the Appeals Board to care about the Chesapeake Bay, for which they are responsible, and to deliberate accordingly.

"Since the disturbance occurred prior to obtaining the proper permits, resulting in damages that permits would have prevented, I believe the only proper corrective action of Wicomico County and the State of Maryland to bring the disturbance into compliance with the Chesapeake Bay Critical Area Law is to deny the variance, deny the permits, order mitigation and the removal of all structures, fine the violator and thank Mr. Lewis for the opportunity to send a strong and clear message to anyone who is considering following in his footsteps: 'If you want to disregard laws, go play somewhere else.'"

The Board of Zoning Appeals rejected Lewis' request for a variance. But since money is no obstacle to the wealthy sportsman, his attorneys initiated what would prove to be a three-year battle through the Maryland court system, losing each skirmish in turn until the case finally reached the Maryland Court of Appeals. There, in a four-to-three decision, the public learned a hard lesson once again: Being seated on a bench—even a high bench—does not insure that a judge will be bound to uphold either the law or the public interest.

Judge Dale R. Cathell articulated the majority decision, which returned the Lewis case to the Wicomico County Board of Zoning Appeals for reconsideration. Central to Cathell's thinking appears to be the contention that since Wicomico County failed to prove that demonstrable harm resulted from Lewis' actions, his request for a variance should be favorably considered.

Does it mean, I wonder, that if I were brought before the honorable judge for speeding through his hometown, running every traffic light and stop sign along the way, that he would exonerate me if my arresting officer couldn't prove that I caused harm in the process?

Cathell raises the absurd fear that enforcement of the Critical Area Act will close the Chesapeake and its entire watershed to development. He also apparently believes that Lewis should not have to suffer the unwarranted hardship that everyone else endures by having to travel from their beds to the marsh where they want to hunt. Nor should he be penalized, the jurist suggests, just because he failed to apply for building, well and septic permits. The arguments are too ludicrous for a response.

"Oblivious to virtually every regulation of federal, state and local law," dissenting Judge Alan M. Wilner wrote in his opinion, "Lewis promptly began destroying vegetation and constructing buildings, all without a permit, all without notice, all in secret, all illegally."

How can one jurist see so clearly and another be so blind?

After many hours of legal debate during February, March and April 2004, the Wicomico County Board of Zoning Appeals again rejected Edwin Lewis' variance request, and Lewis' attorneys have initiated another appeal of the decision. As this book goes to press, the matter is again working its way through the Maryland courts. Regardless of the eventual outcome, we can be certain of one thing: This will not be the last attack on Delmarva's last wild river.

If there is a ditch on or near your property that flows into a branch or stream that eventually empties into the Nanticoke River, you live in the Nanticoke watershed, and activities on your property can have a direct effect on the health and vitality of the river. Land owners in the greater Nanticoke watershed who are interested in learning more about how they can preserve or restore their land and contribute to the health of the river can begin by going to the website www.nanticokeriver.org/resour2.html and contacting some of the resources listed there, such as the Chesapeake Bay Foundation, the Maryland and Delaware Departments of Natural Resources, the Center for Watershed Restoration or American Rivers.

Regardless of where you live, you are in or near the watershed of some river, and all watersheds and rivers desperately need our help. It is an issue that requires everyone's attention and commitment to do what is best for us and all that will follow. Get involved! Save a river!

The Legend
of Wish Sheppard

O n July 15, 1915, while walking through a strip of woods near her home in Caroline County, Maryland, fifteen-year-old Mildred Clark was threatened at the point of a revolver by a young man, who then dragged her into a thicket, sexually assaulted her and fled.

Within minutes of the girl's report, alarms were sounded in Federalsburg. More than a hundred armed citizens spread out over the countryside in search of the attacker, and Sheriff Temple was summoned from the county seat in Denton. The law officer soon arrested a number of suspects but released them when Clark failed to find her assailant among them. The following day Temple brought in Wish Sheppard, who had previously been arrested for stealing five cents on one occasion and later served eighteen months in the Maryland House of Correction for the theft of a bicycle. The girl immediately identified him.

Understanding the hostile mood in Federalsburg, the sheriff promptly loaded his prisoner and started for Denton. Word of the arrest spread quickly, however, and several carloads of men gave chase, intent on lynching Sheppard, but failed to overtake Temple and his prisoner.

That week's edition of the *Denton Journal* carried the following headline: "THE BLACK BRUTE IS CAUGHT—Wish Sheppard, Who Attacked Miss Clark, Is In Jail."

"The excitement and indignation at Federalsburg and in the whole section thereabout," reported the *Journal*, "is still manifest, and to avoid an uprising and attack on the jail, it is said a speedy trial will be ordered by the court."

A reporter described Mildred Clark as being "a very attractive girl with pretty features and a refined manner." The words he used to characterize the accused would be quickly censured if they appeared in a newspaper today: "He is a Negro about twenty years old, of exceedingly repulsive features, with very thick, protruding lips, flat nose and retreating forehead, his big, bold, rolling eyes being conspicuous by the white in them, suggesting brutish instincts."

Sheppard was said to have confessed his guilt to the sheriff in route to Denton and to a second official after being incarcerated.

As threats against Sheppard's life increased, Temple moved his prisoner to the Baltimore City Jail for safekeeping. Then, on Sunday morning, July 25, he returned to the city with a deputy and secretly transported Sheppard back to Denton at nightfall.

The trial began on Monday morning with Judges Constable, Adkins and Hopper on the bench. Hundreds of automobiles and carriages had arrived in Denton, and more than two thousand eager spectators jammed the corridors and grounds of the courthouse. When the door to the courtroom was finally opened, the crowd defied directions to enter singly and overran the bailiffs, boisterously filling every square foot of the room.

The ugly mood finally subsided after the sheriff and his deputies presented themselves and Judge Constable addressed the mob, informing them that the hall would be cleared if order was not restored and maintained.

Procedures commenced with a reading of the indictment, to which Sheppard entered a plea of "not guilty," then chose to be tried by the court rather than a jury.

To protect the girl from embarrassment, the judges moved Mildred Clark and three women who had witnessed her condition immediately after the assault to a jury room, where their testimony was taken only in the presence of Sheppard and counsel from both sides. The court then recessed for lunch.

In the afternoon session, Dr. G. F. Galloway, who had attended Miss Clark after the attack, gave testimony about the child's physical injuries in open court. Others presented evidence that Sheppard had been in the immediate vicinity about the time of the crime and had been traced back to Federalsburg. Tracks found in the road and across the fields corresponded to the size of Sheppard's shoes. After the court overruled objections to admitting the prisoner's confession, it adjourned for the day.

A crowd of several hundred gathered on Denton's public square that evening when a rumor was circulated that the court had agreed on a prison sentence for Sheppard rather than execution. Plans to storm the jail were openly discussed and hysteria spread throughout the region.

News that Sheppard was going to be lynched reached Cambridge shortly after midnight, and several carloads of men set out to witness the event. Between Federalsburg and Williamsburg, one car skidded on a patch of sand and crashed into a telephone pole, killing George E. Lee, Jr. and injuring three others.

Feelings remained at a fever pitch in Denton until State's Attorney Owens circulated through the excited crowd and assured everyone that the case was not finished and that justice would be served. Gradually, the attitude of the demonstrators changed, and the majority began to disperse, singing "Tipperary" and firing pistol shots in the air as they left the green. Law officers and specially deputized citizens surrounded the jail until daybreak, but the tumult had completely vanished by sunrise.

Tuesday began in court with testimony about Sheppard's confessions and continued with witnesses presenting a progression of evidence concerning the defendant's whereabouts on the day of the assault.

After the state rested its case, Sheppard's attorney offered a sworn statement by Wish's mother that provided an alibi for her son, and several young black men gave testimony to support Mrs. Sheppard's claim. One swore that a strange man fitting Sheppard's description had been observed in town the night before the attack on Miss Clark. No other witness could be found to corroborate his story, and two Federalsburg residents testified that the witness had given identical unsupported testimony in a similar case a few years earlier.

When Sheppard was put on the stand, he said he didn't know his age but thought he was eighteen and had lived in Federalsburg all his life. He denied that he had been on the same side of the river as Miss Clark on July15 and said he knew nothing of the attack until his mother told him. He denied having made a confession.

Testimony ended at four o'clock and closing arguments were brief. Court was adjourned before six with an announcement by the judges that they would reassemble at eight to render their decision. A crowd began to gather about seven o'clock and the mood was tense.

An awesome stillness came over the courtroom as the judges returned and took their seats. Speaking in a strong, clear voice, Judge Constable congratulated the Caroline County citizens on their general respect for the law, then gravely admonished those present against unruly demonstrations of either approval or disapproval of the decision that was about to be rendered. He then pronounced Sheppard guilty and instructed the prisoner to stand. Sheppard was asked whether he had anything to say before sentence was passed. He said he did not. The prisoner had been generally indifferent throughout the proceedings.

"You elected to be tried by the judges," Constable began. "We have paid strict attention to all that has been said. We have taken into consideration the statement of witnesses and yourself, and we have sifted the evidence for and against you. We have ruled out the confession credited to you. The court has arrived at its conclusion solely by the evidence presented. It is not a pleasant task to impose the punishment that must fit this crime, and that punishment is death. There is not much I can say to you, except to advise you that you have yet time to prepare yourself during your last few days on earth. There is no use rehearsing the evidence adduced at this trial. Your days will be shortened, and I advise you to seek the counsel of some of the holy ministers of the Gospel. You are to be retuned to the Caroline County Jail and there confined until such time as the governor of this state shall issue your death warrant, and the sentence of this court is that you shall be hanged by the neck until you are dead. And may God have mercy on your soul."

As might be expected, crowds awaiting the court's decision received the news with great approval, and cheers rose from the streets of Denton.

The following editorial note appeared in the next edition of the *Journal*: "The circumstance and publicity of the punishment of the scaffold ought to be known to every one of his type, whose presence in any community is a menace and a curse—a menace and a curse, which when known, will not be allowed to long remain. The red blood of the Caucasian has ever demanded the life of the perpetrator for such defilement of womanhood, and this is the fiat, which nothing can ever change. But it is far better for the public when the law can make prompt disposition of such vile cumberers of the earth."

While Sheppard was awaiting execution, his ten-year-old brother, Rex, was charged with stealing ice cream. "The state's attorney will likely have him sent to some institution," the *Journal* reported on August 14, then followed up seven days later with an announcement that he had been sent to a "Negro reform school at Cheltenham, Md., as incorrigible."

The gallows for Sheppard's execution was borrowed from Baltimore County, and Sheriff Temple announced that the public would be denied access to the event. Only relatives of the prisoner who wished to be present, physicians, officers, ministers and members of the press would be permitted to witness the execution.

The wooden framework was first erected in the carriage house on the jail grounds, but after hundreds of people had viewed the setting, it was moved outside, next to the barn. Under the direction of the Baltimore County warden, tests were conducted with a sandbag to insure that the trap would drop on the pull of a lever.

On the evening preceding Sheppard's death, two pastors and four women conducted religious services and sang hymns in his cell. Other prisoners in the jail joined the chorus that could be heard across the Choptank River and a mile away. "One of the other prisoners—a Ridgely Negro called 'Spider,'" a reporter wrote, "has a baritone voice that would be worth a fortune to some men."

Sheppard, it was claimed, showed little interest in his visitors, and one of the preachers said he believed the prisoner to be "not more than half-witted." Guards claimed that he slept soundly after the services.

On August 27, 1915, forty-three days after the assault on Mildred Clark, the condemned man woke early. He ordered breakfast but did not eat. "He was dressed for the death scene," the *Journal* reported (Sheppard had been given a suit for his execution), "and with a firm step accompanied the officers and his spiritual advisers to the scaffold by the side of the marsh, walking undismayed through the throng which had assembled in the early dawn along the way from the prison to the gallows, his big eyes rolling fearlessly around, surveying the people who watched the procession moving. On the scaffold, Deputy Sheriff Lord asked Sheppard if he had a last word to say, and he replied he had not as the black cap was adjusted. Then he told Mr. Lord he would like to speak with his girl. Informed that it was then too late, he said, 'All right.' Sheriff Temple moved the lever, and the black-shrouded body of the young Negro shot down as the trap fell and he was dead almost instantly, for there was scarcely any struggle. Once or twice his shoulders writhed."

The time was 6:00 a.m.

An undertaker's assistant from Federalsburg removed Sheppard's body and transported it to his mother's home in an automobile.

The hanging of Sheppard was the first legal execution in Caroline since that of Shelby Jump in 1822, and it was also the last, but there were three lynchings in the interim: Dave Thomas, who was hanged in a barn, and Jim Wilson and Marshall Price, who were each dragged from the Denton Jail by a mob and hanged to a tree in the vicinity of the courthouse. Wilson's body was also dismembered and burned.

On September 4, 1915, the following note appeared in the Denton newspaper: "Hangman's ropes come rather high. There is evidently a fictitious value placed upon them, although they are much better than the ordinary hemp rope. The one that was used in the hanging of Wish Sheppard cost $25. The bill for it was before the county commissioners on Tuesday last."

But that is not the end of the story. Those associated with the Caroline County Detention Center have insisted over the years that the ghost of Wish Sheppard haunts its passageways. Some of the stories have been recorded in *Voices from the Land: A Caroline County Memoir*—an oral history collected by Mary Anne Fleetwood, edited by Betty Carroll Callahan and published by the Caroline County Historical Society.

Sheriff Louis Andrew was ten when he came to live in the jail. His father was sheriff and sheriffs' families were housed on the premises. He succeeded his father in 1961. "The prisoners have got me up at three o'clock in the morning," he was quoted in the 1980s, "telling me there was something in that jail. I'd take a flashlight and look in each corner to show 'em there wasn't anybody but themselves in the jail. Yet they said they could hear these footsteps come by 'em. One man had scratches all over his arms and face. He swore to me that none of the inmates did it.

"I've had one boy beat the door so bad that he was shaking when I got to him. He said, 'Sheriff, you got to let me in with the other prisoners,' and the next morning he was lying right beside the bed with 'em, scared to death. He said, 'The ghost was there, walking around.' Sometimes, the prisoners say he pulls the pants off of 'em or pulls their shirts or watches off.

"I had a woman in jail one time, and she told me I was pulling a chain up and down the steps trying to scare her at four in the morning. I had to convince her it wasn't me pulling the chain.

"I had an old man in here one time. He was seventy-five years old. He would tell me: 'Sheriff, there's no ghost in here. It's just a bunch of them boys.' I said, 'Charlie, you're right.' One night, Charlie got to beating on the door. He said, 'Sheriff, I got to take all that back. He's here. He's come to my room tonight.'

"Most of the prisoners has never seen him. They just hear foot-steps. They'll swing at him, but they can't hit nothing. It's just the ghost."

Legend claims that Wish Sheppard left a handprint on the wall of his cell when officers led him off to the gallows. Sheriff Andrew was asked about the story and said, "There is a handprint on the wall of Wish Sheppard's old cell. I painted over it several times since I've been here, but it comes back. I put cement across it and it's come back. The legend is he put his hands on the wall to hold his-self back when he was carried out to be hung. The handprint is on the wall of the old part of the jail. When they remodeled the jail in 1981-1982, they left the door that Wish Sheppard come out of, and as far as I know, that door has not been opened since 1938."

The jail was remodeled again in 1996 and the section containing Sheppard's old cell was gutted. Nothing remains. I spoke to Warden Charles Andrew, Louis' son, in September 2004 and asked if any-thing had been observed on the wall when the cell had been opened. "No," he replied, "but I will tell you this: The door to the cell was welded shut, and it had a little trap door into it. When the worker was removing it, the trap door opened and hit him on the leg. He said it was Wish Sheppard.

"I have correction officers who swear he's here. One of the dis-patchers saw the image of a man in the window at the 911 center one night, and it scared him. He said he was ready to climb into the radio.

"We had a swinging gate back in the '80s, and the gate would start swinging right by itself. They would look to see if it was a dep-uty playing a game on them. Nothing! But it would swing.

"There's an elevator here, and the elevator will run from floor to floor by itself—nobody on it.

"There's an intercom at every door throughout the jail. One night, the outside intercom to the recreation yard kept coming on. This was two o'clock in the morning and the officer knew there was nobody out there, but he sent somebody to check. There's a button you push, and a light will come on and a bell will ring. It kept doing that several more times and then it stopped.

"Officers will say they go up a flight of steps and get that cold feeling. They'll say, 'Wish, you live here and I've got to work here. Let's get along.' And inmates say that weird things go on."

And so the legend of Wish Sheppard has entered a new millennium and will survive, I feel certain, for as long as there is a Caroline County.

The Hanging of Wish Sheppard

More Nanticoke Books
Folks and Tales from Delmarva

Conversations in a Country Store by Hal Roth—How things used to be on Delmarva; Paperback; $12.95

You Can't Never Get to Puckum by Hal Roth—Delmarva history, folks and folklore; Paperback; $12.95

The Monster's Handsome Face by Hal Roth—Facts and fiction about Patty Cannon, Delmarva's most notorious kidnapper and murderer; Hardbound; $19.95

You Still Can't Get to Puckum by Hal Roth—Delmarva history, folks and folklore; Paperback; $14.95

The Entailed Hat by George Alfred Townsend—A novel set in the early 19th century about kidnapping, murder and romance on Delmarva; Paperback, $16.95

In Days Gone By by Hal Roth—Delmarva history, folks and folklore; Paperback; $12.95

Stories of the Eastern Shore by John Hill—Growing up on Delmarva in the nineteenth century; Paperback; $7.95

Road Rage and Rummage Sales by Helen Chappell—Short stories; Paperback; $10.95

Two Pieces of Clothes by Hal Roth—Oral history of elderly African Americans on Delmarva; paperback; $12.95

Washington Book Distributors
4930-A Eisenhower Avenue
Alexandria, VA 22304
Phone: 1-800-699-9113—Fax: 703-212-9114
E-mail: washbook@juno.com
www.washingtonbk.com/